BECOMING A MAVEN

A Guide to Remember & Embrace
Your Magic Through Spiritual
Self-Awareness

Ruth Montgomery

Becoming a Maven
A Guide to Remember & Embrace Your Magic
Through Spiritual Self-Awareness

Copyright © 2024 by Ruth Montgomery

ISBN: 978-1-7382334-0-3

Published by: The Maven Project
www.themavenproject.ca

Published in Ontario, Canada

DEDICATION

To all of my soul sisters and brothers, my family,
the significant characters in my story who have taught me so
many lessons, my clients and community of mavens.
Thank you.

To you, the reader, "All you need is faith, trust and
a little pixie dust." Peter Pan

...because we all need to believe in something.
Whatever that looks like. It is yours to believe in.
Consider this your pixie dust to believe in yourself;
in the maven that you are,
and in the maven that you are becoming.

CONTENTS

PREFACE

When I started on this journey of personal development, I didn't mean to, and frankly, I didn't even know it had begun until I was in it. I have always sought out experiences and have always enjoyed learning from different people – hearing their stories and being immersed in their cultures. Through my travels over the years, I have questioned why as humans (when our basic needs are the same; food, water, shelter) are we so different? I began to wonder, how were there so many influences on how we functioned through life? Around the world and even in our communities. And how many of those influences were actually ones I agreed with?

Do you remember in high school, learning about Maslow's Hierarchy of Needs? In high school, the concept was beyond what I could truly comprehend. Yes, I could study, and memorize it, but it wasn't until much later, that I could truly speak or live it. As I write this, it's a moment that I realize had more impact than I've maybe understood until now. How many of those moments have created who we are? Moments, tidbits of knowledge, passing comments from a friend or stranger that have made us pause and think "hmm, there's something there. I'm not sure what to do with it, but I know it's significant".

Maslow's Theory recognized that we needed to feel fulfilled in each level of the triangle; starting with the foundation, before we could move to the next layer in our human experience. Often we are searching for self-actualization thinking our purpose will make everything else fall into place, when in reality, you need to build yourself up to that. By first creating relationships, a sense of belonging, self-confidence and self-esteem, purpose will follow.

After high school I had no idea what I wanted to do as an 18-year-old and was searching for that ever-elusive purpose. I decided to follow my love of design to study Interior Design in Canada and went on to obtain a Master's Degree of Design Futures in Australia. This degree was a moment of significance I wasn't able to understand at the time, but it sparked something. Design Futures is about design responsibility, and how as a designer we should be aware that everything we put into the world has a life beyond its designed life. From the perspective of sustainability, physical products get disposed of and are sourced from materials around the world. Therefore, we need to be conscious creators in this world as we bring more into existence.

Designs are also brought into this world with an intended purpose. Yet, as the designed item lives and breathes in the world, it evolves and shifts, suddenly creating or adapting to its new environment. It can even start to shift human behaviour. The car for instance, was created as a mode of transportation. A novelty item at the time, it immediately created a divide between who could afford the car and who could not. Here we had a glimpse into upper, middle and lower class. The creation process initiated the assembly line manufacturing system, which led to people doing repetitive tasks over and over all day long. The manufacturers recognized this, and offered higher salaries to compensate for the lack of job satisfaction; a system many people still live by today. Fast forward to now, look around you – every single item in your home has most likely been in or on a vehicle at some point during its lifecycle. Everything. Our cities, our access to food and medical care are designed now based on road access – relying heavily on the vehicle. That one simple design, has evolved an entire world.

During my Master's Degree, we were studying a lot of philosophical and psychological texts, and the idea of "enlightenment" started to be tossed around. Other students were having an awakening or being referred to as "awake" but I wasn't understanding it. It was a term that meant so much, but was unfortunately, explained so poorly. When I'd ask fellow students or my professors, they didn't have the language to put it into words. I kept hearing, "when you're enlightened or going through an awakening you just know". Well, how the hell am I supposed to know if I'm going through it or experiencing it, if I don't know what "it" is? What does it look like, what happens, what do you learn, how can you get there faster? A million questions and no answers. The texts we were reading felt overwhelming and over my head at times, yet this was the required material at the level I was at. It felt like I should have been able to read it; and further, to comprehend it. What a mind game we put ourselves through. It was again one of those moments, where I knew, "there's something to this, I don't quite get it yet, but I'm going to tuck it away for later".

Fast forward a few years, (having moved on from trying to truly understand enlightenment) I started diving into self-help and business leadership type books. I was unhappy working for someone else, and struggling to find a job I loved. I started working with a network marketing company, because, like a lot of people, I was not satisfied in the typical constraints of the job that I had studied so hard to get. I was looking for that missing piece.

I started attending business conferences and personal development workshops knowing there had to be more. I wanted to live a fulfilled life, but how? Almost everyone around me was doing the exact same thing, living day to day within their routines – some extremely happy, and others seem to have settled, having given up the search to find anything more.

I was looking for real life examples of how to live a fulfilled life, or what that even looked like *to me*. It was here that some of the books or podcasts my mentors started suggesting, felt like I was reading Shakespeare for the first time. It was like trying to understand a foreign film, without subtitles. I could feel that it was powerful. I knew in my body that these were important lessons, yet I didn't have the tools to make sense of it all. Again, I was feeling discouraged, and feeling like I was missing something.

Around this time, I also decided to venture into the world of Entrepreneurship as an Interior Designer and Professional Organizer. It was in exploring this that I realized how lonely entrepreneurship can be which inspired the initial stages of my business The Maven Project. A project inspired to offer workshops for like-minded entrepreneurs.

I chose the business name because maven, by definition is "one who is experienced or knowledgeable", aka: an expert. It's also derived from the Yiddish word, "meyvn" which means "one who understands".

A **maven** is also described as an expert who seeks to pass knowledge onto others. A term which we all deserve to use and define ourselves as. We are all experts at something, we all have a knowledge base that is unique to our life and experiences. It is not defined, necessarily, by our job title or our education. It goes beyond that. It goes into each moment of your life; the ups, the downs, and every experience that you have had. Every conversation that has made you pause, every emotion you've felt and every interaction you've observed. Becoming A Maven is about taking all of those moments of your life that have brought you here to this book. It is about being able to step back and understand that without those moments you would not be who you are today. Each piece has shaped or shifted you into the maven that you are. And for that I am forever grateful.

Being a maven means standing in your power and in your story *and* embracing every aspect of it. Taking all of the little pieces and putting it together to be your true self. All of it. Showing up as you; honest, vulnerable and whole. And sharing that knowledge with others, if you so choose.

The Maven Project evolved into retreats, and our most popular event, Camp Maven. A women's only summer camp inspired to bring women together to re-connect to their inner child; to be a kid again, and to return to that childlike state of bliss!

Personal development is like learning any new skill, it takes hours of practice, and mistakes. It takes courage in putting yourself into a room with people you admire, knowing you're not at their level, *yet*. It takes resilience in seeking out opportunities, *and* creating opportunities. It takes vulnerability to be completely raw and real, and to truly see yourself.

Slowly, you learn to be okay with all aspects of yourself. And eventually, you learn to love yourself fully. You start to see the moments as lessons, and the people as teachers. You start to see the maven that you have been all along. It takes time to peel back the layers of what society has told you; of who you should be, do or have. To unlearn the beliefs that outside influences had you believing. To truly step into yourself and to see that each of us are mavens, unique and individual in all that we are.

The Maven Project continues to evolve, and now more than ever recognizing that the pieces of our story are exactly that – pieces to a bigger puzzle. My path to get here is all connected. Each lesson, or moment that I have picked up over the years, has made me who I am today. Over the years, I have had many moments asking, who am I to share this work? When the real question is, who am I not to?

Through this book, I will thread those pieces together showing you how you can do the same. Using my love of design, my unique gift of understanding the deeper meaning of surface level experiences, and my ability to inspire you to believe in yourself – I hope this book helps you to see the maven that you are. To remind you of all that you know, and to allow you the space to create more self-awareness.

The journey of Becoming a Maven is a journey of remembering and returning to who you truly are. Of reflecting inward to get to know yourself, to create self-sovereignty and to find the freedom to be yourself.

I am writing this book to offer a translation into the world of personal and spiritual development. To help guide you through these initial stages of Becoming a Maven. Offering you an insight into the language, into some of the tools available and the ideas that are shared across the realms of personal development. Because the more and more I read and learn from others, the more and more I understand we are all saying similar things. Some people are saying it in a language that our soul understands, and some are planting seeds of importance for us to return to once we've picked up a few extra lessons. The intention behind this book is to help you recognize that you have magic within you. Everything you are seeking by doing this work is already within you, I am just here to help you remember and embrace it!

Thank you for being here. In this world, reading this book, and as the maven that you are.

With so much love,

P.S. Please note, that this book is written from my experience growing up in Canada with a Western perspective. This book offers an introduction into many very sacred processes and all are written through the lens of my experience. Each practice is different and many cultures and/or religions have their own unique perspective. Start to explore and try different versions for yourself to see what resonates with your individual journey. Trust that you will be guided to the right retreats, classes and teachers along the way.

PHASE ONE

CURIOSITY

"Every nature, every modeled form,
every creature, exists in and with each other."

Mary Magdalene

Self-Improvement is really a growing into or of oneself. You don't need to improve. You are whole as you are now. However, there is always a knowing of self that is going to get deeper. A self-growth as you become aware. Nothing *needs* to change, but it naturally will as you evolve into knowing yourself better. Like any relationship deepens and expands, the one with yourself is often the hardest to understand, but it is the most important relationship you will ever have.

You didn't get here without a little curiosity and a knowing that there is something more you are seeking to learn or understand. If you are reading this book, know that you are in the right place. The right teachers and lessons come into our lives at the perfect moment. This is your reminder to trust those nudges, always.

Curiosity is the teacher that we all have access to no matter what our current situation is. It shows up in those moments that spark excitement, the moments that make your eyes sparkle or your belly twirl. The moments when you get full body goosebumps. When you just "know", and you don't know why.

It's the internal teacher that nudges us to ask more questions, to explore an option and to follow up when something jumps out at us. Have you ever had a conversation with someone, and they're telling you about their day, and a totally irrelevant point in the story piques your interest? That's curiosity telling you to follow up with that. To ask why did that particular thing, whether it was a person, place or activity, jump out of the thousands of other words your friend said? Why that particular thing?

Or when you learn about something new one day, and then hear about it from different sources again in the next few days. It is your curiosity that nudges you to listen, to follow it, and to explore.

Throughout this journey of becoming a maven, I want you to explore it with the curiosity of a child. When we were children, we did things simply because we wanted to. Before society told us who we *should* be, how we *should* act and what we *should* do. Before we felt the need to explain ourselves or have a motive for doing something - we simply were.

Follow your curiosity. Piece by piece. Let it guide you as you feel called and if something I say or share here, doesn't resonate with you – leave it. Only take what you feel drawn to, and leave the rest. When something here inspires you, makes you pause or causes your body to react – follow that with passion!

Human Experience

"You are an infinite spiritual being having
a temporary human experience."

Dr. Wayne W. Dyer

In a world where we are so connected digitally, we are more disconnected from others and ourselves than ever before. Technology is a beautiful creation, but it's easy to get sucked in and distracted. And that's kind of the point; to distract us further from ourselves – but that's a whole other conversation.

We are physically here on Earth as spiritual beings, here to have a human experience. We are here to experience our bodies, our surroundings, and the connection of other humans.

We are born into a body, our physical vessel. We are here in this realm to experience life on Earth. To experience all of our senses, to embrace our learnings and our lessons. Being human is all we know, for a large part of our life.

As a child we come into this world and we mirror those around us. We learn from what others are doing and we start to see how to act as a human. We start to pick up habits and ideologies from the people and the places near us. We start to see where we fit in, within the world around us. We can morph into a version of ourselves we no longer recognize as we try so hard to fit in. Throughout this book, I want to remind you that there is no room for self-criticism or judgement. Everything we are learning here is from a lens of love and compassion – have compassion for yourself and give yourself so much love as we start to dive in.

> "Too often we listen to what the world around us is saying.
> We've distanced ourselves from ourselves so much that
> we don't even know who we are anymore. But you do.
> It's inside of you. You just have to listen."

Ruth Montgomery, March 2020 Journal Entry

Stepping into the world of personal or spiritual development can feel so daunting, because we've come so far from ourselves. This world of personal development is about learning who we are again, at our core. It opens us up to truly seeing ourselves as the beautiful and imperfect beings that we are, and teaches us to love every piece of that. This work isn't always easy, but I promise you, it is worth it!

One of the first places to begin to come back to yourself is to start outside of yourself. This may sound counterproductive, but going within right away can be overwhelming. It is easy to give up and shut down if we move too quickly. Let's start with the spaces closest to us and work our way in slowly.

Your Home

The first place we want to explore is your home. This is your sanctuary or safe space from the world. It's where you can truly relax and be yourself. Look at your home, and the spaces that you spend most of your time in. As a designer, and professional organizer, I have worked with a lot of clients who have moved into a home, and kept it exactly as the previous owners had it. Same furniture layout, same wall colour, even using the same nails that photos had hung on previously. No judgement here if you're looking around and thinking, 'she's talking about me'!

If your house has been beautifully designed and nurtured, then it may feel wonderful, but it's important to check in with yourself. We can start with: does this feel like *your* home? Does it feel like you're living in someone else's house? Are you scared to move things around or to try something new?

A tell-tale sign that your house isn't working the way it is set up is if there is clutter. The physical clutter around you leads to an emotional inner chaos – *or* does the emotional inner chaos lead to the physical clutter? It's kind of a chicken and egg scenario, in that we don't know which came first. The physical clutter around us, often represents or mirrors what internally we know, but maybe can't quite express externally.

It can be that feeling of there's so much to do, or the claustrophobic feelings of being trapped in your life, or current situation. It can show up in that feeling of overwhelm when you don't understand why or where it is coming from. Look around you. Does your physical space resemble what you are feeling internally?

That correlation is often so close to us, it's easy to miss. The energy and space in our homes speak louder than we realize, and because we're so used to it, we rarely take the time to re-evaluate. What is happening in your space (the physical areas you spend time in) influences, and can act as a mirror for, how you are feeling.

When we can't control something bigger than ourselves, it is often reflected in our homes. Your home is your sacred space. It is the one thing in your life, when you are seeking to re-gain control of your life and of who you are, that's constant. It's the one space you can control, even if everything else feels out of control, because it's yours.

It's your home, *it* belongs to you. You don't belong to it. What is happening in your space around you is what you are subconsciously allowing to happen to you externally. Start to look around and see what is and isn't working. We're going to break it down, focusing on one room at a time. Take this section as slowly as you need. You don't need to change anything today, and you don't need to change everything all at once. These are ideas and suggestions on how to make your space better reflect the maven that you are – take all of them with curiosity and see what resonates.

11

Where you Rest Your Body:

You spend approximately 8 hours a day in your bedroom, which means 30% of your life is spent in this room. Does it look like a space where you want to spend one third of your day? Does it feel like a relaxing space to gain rest?

Your bedroom should be a place where you can undress and feel fully you. You should feel luxurious, and beautiful as you get your "beauty rest". This is the place where you are revitalizing your body every day.

When I was staying at my parents recently, I journaled: "I couldn't sleep at my parents and was feeling so much anxiety about how much I had to do. It felt like a ticking time bomb. I woke up to the clock ticking above me. I took out the batteries and was able to sleep peacefully." Such a simple thing that felt so insignificant, actually caused so much stress. Notice your surroundings, and notice what you're drawn to or irritated by. There are clues there as to the simple changes you can start to make.

Looking at the overall feel of your bedroom, start to ask what is it reflecting to your body and the world around you. For instance, if you are constantly watching television before bed long past when you become tired, that's the energy you are subconsciously telling your body is okay for you. You are saying 'you don't deserve proper rest and waking up exhausted is just part of life'. Or if your bedroom is dreary, and unexciting, I'd be asking: how is your sex life and libido? Is this a room that says luxury and pleasure? Or a room that says mediocre and boring is acceptable?

Does your bedroom have used sheets or items from a past relationship? Does their energy linger in *your* personal bedroom? If you are currently single, it can emit an energy that says that sacred space is already taken and filled with someone else. If you are having marital or relationship problems and seem to bicker in the bedroom, perhaps notice if there are past memories subconsciously entering into your space.

If this is the case, try removing anything from a past relationship out of the bedroom. It doesn't mean you need to get rid of it completely, but the bedroom should be your sacred place. If you are looking for a new romantic partner create the physical space to let the energetic space expand and open up. And if you have a current romantic partner, the bedroom should bring you both the same joy. Encourage your partner to be a part of the process of creating the oasis that you both desire in your bedroom.

An Extra Dose of Magic

A few things to notice as you look around your bedroom:

- Do you work from bed? Do you find yourself thinking about work when you are trying to sleep? *Your body may not know how to separate the two, and this can create an imbalance of work-life priorities. Try to keep the bedroom only for sleep and relaxing or intimate experiences.*

- Do you have a tv on constantly? How is your quality of sleep? *If you are allowing other stimulation such as sound and light to be going on when your body is trying to focus on sleep, it may be distracted and your sleep will be disrupted subconsciously. Try turning off the tv and shutting the blinds before you go to sleep.*

- Are there visible piles of dirty laundry? *There may be a running to-do list going on in your mind, creating a feeling of overwhelm. Try containing the dirty laundry in a hamper, giving your mind a clean, uninterrupted scan of the room, which will create a sense of peace.*

- How old are your sheets, comforter or duvet? Are your pillows or mattress tired and uncomfortable? *This quality indicates the quality you are telling your body you deserve and in turn can affect your connection to feelings of worthiness. Where else is this lack of worthiness showing up in your life? Please note: if it is a decision or not a priority (either financial or aesthetic wise) then you are deciding that it is okay for now. Your body knows it is a choice because you value that quality to show up in other areas of your life first right now – and that's okay. When it is not by choice, but by habit, it creates a misinformed subconscious belief within the body. The focus here is creating awareness.*

- When was the last time you cleaned your sheets? *Often this is something we don't think about until we're crawling into bed, and we think, I'll do it tomorrow. Where else are you delaying what you deserve and desire in your life by putting yourself at the end of the day?*
- Do you wake up feeling refreshed and ready for the day? Or tired and exhausted? *Notice what your room reflects – does the paint feel tired and old, does the flooring need a good clean? This is where we spend the majority of our time – we want this space to feel fresh and clean!*

Where You Clean Your Body:

Moving into your bathroom, this is where you get yourself ready for the day and where you take care of your body. It is also where you see your body in all of its naked glory!

If your bathroom feels overwhelming with too many options and products – how are you at making decisions? If every morning you start your day faced with so many options, are you choosing the product that actually works for you? Or are you settling and grabbing the first one you see, because it's "good enough"? Are there other areas of your life where you are settling because it's good enough?

Remove, donate or throw out any products that you don't or will not use. Be honest with yourself. If it's expired or you haven't used it in the last 6 months, chances are it can go! If throwing out perfectly good products feels terrible, call your local women's or homeless shelter and see if they are accepting donations. A lot of those products would be greatly appreciated by someone else!

An Extra Dose of Magic

A few things to notice as you look around your bathroom:

- Is your bathroom tidy? *Tidy shows up as a sense of order in other forms of our life. So, notice when you start keeping your spaces tidy how the drama in your life starts to dissipate.*

- Is your bathroom clean and in proper working condition? *Clean can appear in our world, as lingering problems. If you are keeping the space clean, you are saying to the world I want simplicity and ease. It creates a flow to allow our desires to show up more easily. How can we see what we desire or what opportunities are there for us if the window we are looking through is dirty? Or how can we expect opportunities to flow to us if the drain is always clogged?*
- Do you have a million products taking up space, when you really only use a couple of favourites? *This often shows up within our ability to make decisions for ourselves. And our ability to take on too much. Where in your life have you said yes when what you really wanted to say was no?*
- Are your towels plush and cozy feeling? Or starting to resemble worn-out rags? *Each time you shower, you wrap yourself in these towels. This can show up as worthiness. Where else are you feeling a lack of worthiness, or that you only deserve a certain level of quality?*

Where You Relax Your Body:

Looking at your living area or space where you relax. This is where you unwind after a long day, and where you spend quality time with your loved ones.

Notice here, are you able to relax? If there is always something out that "needs to be done", do you feel that you *need* to be doing things all of the time to feel worthy? Does your self-worth get wrapped up in what you accomplish? It's important for your body to rest. Try to put things away by finding a home for them, or create more of an office space for the projects that are ongoing that is out of your line of sight when you are trying to relax.

An Extra Dose of Magic
A few things to notice as you look around your living area:
- Is your living area also your work space? Are there piles of projects or things to do laying around? Is it clean and relaxing to be in? *Like the bedroom, we want to subconsciously create a separation so that your body knows when you are in this space, it is okay to relax and rest.*

- Does everything have a home or designated spot? Are the rest of your family aware of those designated spots? *This is an important note in shared spaces – if you are not the only one living in the home, you are not the only one responsible for putting things away. Try including the family in a quick 10-15 minute tidy at the start or end of the day and put everything in its place. This is a great activity to do so that your family will start to know where things belong rather than assuming someone else will pick up after them.*
- Does your mind wander to all of the other things you "should" be doing when you are trying to rest? *If this is something you struggle with, try creating a designated space for ongoing projects to be kept so that they stay out of the main areas. Or create an ongoing to-get-done list where everyone can see it so that you can write down what you "should" be doing – the act of writing it down, allows our mind to rest knowing that you won't forget it.*

Where You Nourish Your Body:

Your body is a vessel, and what you put into your body fuels it. The kitchen is where you create and consume the food that nourishes your body. Where that energy (in the form of food) is stored and how it is served can also have an effect on your body. Not only on how your body absorbs the nutrients, but also in the energy you emit to the world around you.

For instance, if you use a chipped coffee cup in the morning, you start your day off with that energy. You're telling your body that the broken item is enough for you, indirectly starting your day telling your body that that's all you deserve. If you believe that's all you deserve or expect for yourself, others will believe that's all you deserve too. Do you allow others to treat you with disrespect because that's all you feel you are worthy of? Again, chicken or the egg – which came first? If you're the egg, you can't control what the chicken does. You *can* control what you do though, and see how the chicken responds.

An Extra Dose of Magic

A few things to notice as you look around your kitchen:

- Do you have expired food in your kitchen? Do you have garbage on your counters and in your drawers? *Time to tidy up. The energy in your kitchen will be stale like the expired food. Energy is moving constantly; we want to create spaces where higher vibrational energy can flourish.*

- Are there crumbs on your counter? *Are you leaving crumbs (pieces of your energy everywhere) out in the world? It's exhausting to be everything to everyone and leave fragments of yourself exposed. If you find this to be true, it may be time to pull back your energy and set boundaries for where you spend your time and energy. If you let everyone have pieces of you all the time, all that's left at the end of the day may be crumbs. No wonder you're depleted.*

- When was the last time you cleaned out your refrigerator, your oven, stove, and other major cooking appliances? *This is where we store and cook the food that we will ingest to "nourish" our body. Think about the energy that your food is absorbing before you eat it. There is an energetic layer that your body will have to process or cleanse it.*

- Is everything in good working order? Are your dishes broken or chipped? *Do you think that's all you deserve? Now, there is a difference here between what you can actually afford versus what you are choosing to live with. If you cannot afford new dishes, but are aware that you desire new dishes, you are telling yourself, you desire more, and this is only temporary while you invest in things of higher importance. Or if it is a favourite dish that holds a higher sentimental value, you subconsciously know the value of it. However, if you can afford new dishes, and are choosing not to invest in yourself, that begs the question, of where else are you not investing (time, money, resources) in yourself that you could be?*

- Do you have old appliances that you no longer use or intended to use but never have? Are your cupboards full, with things you no longer need, or have never used? *What other areas of your life does it feel full with things you don't actually want or need? Are you filling every minute of your schedule with things you don't want to do? Or things that you could get someone else to do? Moms, I'm looking to you, are you taking on the mental load of the entire house? Perhaps you can delegate some of those tasks, to the other members of your family so your "cupboards" don't feel so full?*

The habits and behaviours we adapt from our environment mirror into the rest of the decisions and behaviours we make throughout our day. What are you setting as your baseline by what you are allowing or choosing as your norm in your home? Allowing that chaos in your home, says "hey Universe, I can handle chaos." And by living in a messy home, the Universe sees that and thinks, "oh, they like the mess. Let's give them more of that in other areas of their life".

The first step in any of this work, is awareness. Choosing to step outside of your current reality and see things from a different perspective. You don't have to re-do your house overnight. Start with one room at a time. Or even one drawer. Break it down into tiny, manageable steps.

Welcome curiosity into your home, and allow yourself to play with your furniture layouts or to re-arrange the artwork on your walls. Hire an Interior Designer, or a Professional Organizer to help get you started, or to give you inspiration for where to begin. If you are adding to your home and making new décor purchases, buy with intention. Don't add to the clutter simply because you think you need something. Wait, and buy items because you love them. If you do actually need something, then make sure to get rid of whatever it is replacing or to create a place for where the new thing will live. Creating a home that reflects you, happens gradually, and can continue to evolve as you evolve. Let it happen organically where you can.

Watch, as your house starts to become a reflection of yourself, how the rest of your immediate world starts to find the same calmness. Allow the state of your home and life to become filled with more aligned energy.

Psychology of Colour:

Another area of your home to consider is the colours you have chosen for your walls, and furniture. Take a look around, does your space include your favourite colours? The colours that make you feel good?

As we grow through different seasons of our life, we are drawn to different colours based on what we need.

The psychology of colour explains that each colour may inspire or enhance different feelings. Warm colours, such as, reds, oranges and yellow can evoke feelings of heightened emotion, such as passion or anger, to warmth and comfort. Cool colours are the blues, greens and purples which are often more neutral and calming colours. These can also be empowering, or evoke sadness. Each person will respond differently to different colours. You can easily search to see what your colours represent, but know that you are usually drawn to certain colours for a reason. This can be inspired by your current season, or what your energy chakras are needing extra support with.

An Extra Dose of Magic

The Chakras are energy centres in our bodies, each representing a different element of our being. For more information, go to page 99. As a quick guide:

- Your **Root Chakra** is red and represents feeling grounded, safe and secure in your body.
- Your **Sacral Chakra** is orange and represents your creative energy and your ability to birth new ideas or life.
- Your **Solar Plexus** is yellow and represents your self-confidence, and the light you radiate to others.
- Your **Heart Chakra** is green and represents your ability to give and receive love.
- Your **Throat Chakra** is blue and represents your ability to speak your truth and to share your voice.
- Your **Third Eye Chakra** is purple and represents your ability to connect to your psychic abilities and intuitive nature.
- Your **Crown Chakra** is white and represents your ability to connect to Source energy and to know that you are always connected.

Colour is a powerful tool and is often underutilized. People have a full body reaction to colour without even knowing it. Think about different brands that you love, or dislike, and notice what colours you are drawn to in artwork or book covers. There is a whole world of researchers and marketing mavens using colours to influence us on a regular basis.

In *Drunk Tank Pink*, author Adam Alter shares a paper written by Professor Alexander Schauss from *Orthomolecular Psychiatry* showing the intense impact that colour can have on us. Schauss described an experiment where 153 healthy young men, individually, were asked to stare at a piece of cardboard for a full minute – half of the men staring at a deep blue piece, and half staring at a bright pink piece. After one minute, the researcher had the men raise their arms and he applied "just enough downward pressure to force their arms back to their sides." When they recovered their strength, he had them repeat the experiment by staring at the opposite color of cardboard and testing their strength again. Adam shares, "The results were strikingly consistent. All but two of the men were dramatically weaker after staring at the pink cardboard...In contrast, the blue cardboard left their strength intact...The color pink appeared to leave the men temporarily depleted."

Schauss went on to test this theory again, sharing, "At one appearance, filmed for TV, a muscle-bound Mr. California performed several effortless biceps curls but struggled to perform a single curl after staring at the pink cardboard." This study goes on to explain that due to the results, correctional facilities and special holding facilities painted their cells "Drunk Tank Pink", a bubble gum pink colour, and noticed a decrease in aggression from inmates. The pink physically weakened, and calmed them down. This became a phenomenon in the early 1980s, and doctors, psychiatrists, and even bus companies started using it with a notable decrease in vandalism, aggression, and hyperactivity. Football teams and boxers even started using this colour in attempts to pacify their opponents by painting their changerooms pink. If you haven't read, *Drunk Tank Pink,* you should. Adam goes on to explain how this and other similar phenomenon can shape the way we think, feel and behave.

Alternative Energy Practices:

Feng Shui is another great tool when you are looking at your home. It is an ancient Chinese practice that uses energy forces and the natural elements to create flow throughout your home. By utilizing different directions in your home, and clearing energy, you can increase the flow and improve various areas of your life, such as wealth, happiness, and family. This can be used to re-arrange furniture or layouts, and to bring in and work with the elements of wind, fire, water and air. There are a lot of books and articles on this practice, or you can hire a Feng Shui maven to come into your home and offer support.

Geopathic Stress and Water Dowsing is also something to be aware of, especially if you are having trouble sleeping. I am by no means, an expert in this, but there are sometimes water lines and geopathic stress lines running deep within the Earth under our homes. We can't see them, and often won't know they are there. In a state of rest, if you are constantly feeling restless, try moving your bed and sleep facing a different direction or in a different part of your room or home. Some people may not pick anything up at all, but as you tap more and more into your self-awareness, your body may start to be more receptive to the energies around it. Babies are more sensitive to their surroundings as well, because they haven't been as conditioned as us to the world around them. If you have a baby that is having trouble sleeping, you can use Water Dowsing sticks to see if there is running water in the ground beneath their crib keeping them up at night. If so, try moving their crib to a different part of the room.

Make the changes to you that feel obvious, and start to explore, with curiosity, what might make your home feel more aligned over the coming weeks and months. Remember, this is a process, and does not need to happen overnight. Now that your home is starting to feel like a home again, we can take a step inward to Your Body.

Your Body

You have one body in this lifetime. One body that is yours to love and to learn from. We are born with a unique body, specific to the lessons we are here to learn and with the strengths we need to thrive in this lifetime. How we show up in our body, and how we interact with our body, are both vital pieces of connecting to ourselves and creating a new level of self-awareness.

What You Wear:

Let's start with how you show up in the world in your body, by looking at the clothes you wear. Looking at our clothing, and our closets provides insight into how we feel in our body. It's often how we want the world to outwardly see us, which is an internal reflection of how we see ourselves.

An easy way to start with looking at your wardrobe, without feeling overwhelmed, is to hang up or neatly fold all of your clothes so that you can see everything at once. If there's anything that stands out that you no longer like or that you've outgrown, you can get rid of it. Next, hang all of your hangers backwards – that way as you wear clothes and hang them back up you can put them in the correct way. This is an easy visual, so that in 3-6 months you can see what clothes you haven't worn.

If you're feeling inspired and want to take the time, take a day, put on some fun music, and your favourite pair of underwear and start to try on all of your clothes. Going through each item to see what fits, what doesn't, what fabric you like, and what colours look and feel good on you. Do this with the intention that your body is perfect exactly as it is. Right now. There is no need to make any changes. This body, this vessel – is yours, and it is perfect. There's no room for shaming it or feeling guilty for its changes and evolution based on unrealistic beauty standards. This is about loving your body exactly as it is.

As you are starting to be aware of your clothing, and how you are presenting yourself to the world, start to look at yourself in the mirror in each outfit. If it's been a while since you've looked in the mirror or really taken the time to see yourself, we'll go deeper into mirror work later on. For now, stand in front of the mirror to look at the clothes you're wearing specifically. If this is too much, inviting a friend over to go through your closet can be fun! Get their honest, but kind, opinion on how the clothes look on you. This allows you to take the space to really focus on how the clothes make you feel in them.

Try to remind yourself during this to see yourself with so much love. There is no room for criticism or low self-talk today – although we can't ignore this completely, we'll come back to that. This exercise is about how you feel in your clothes, and if that matches how you want the world to see you. Another great shift of perspective is, if your friend was wearing it, would you like their outfit? This allows you to separate yourself from the clothes, and simply look at the outfits.

Be mindful of the language you are using as well. Instead of asking, 'how do I look?' Ask 'how do these clothes look on me?' YOU look beautiful. You *are* beautiful. I don't have to see you to know that! By asking how the clothes look, we allow ourselves to find fault with the clothes instead of with our bodies. Our bodies are perfect just as they are. This exercise is about finding clothes that fit your body and make you feel incredible!

And please, may I remind you that the size of your clothing does not matter. How it fits you (not how you fit in it) and how it feels on you, is what matters. The number is not important, and has no impact on your value or on your worthiness to feel good in your clothes.

If you are feeling completely disconnected from your current wardrobe, keep staple items. Shirts and pants that fit, in solid colours. Keep pieces that you love, and with the basics covered you can slowly add in pieces that feel good. Again, like home décor, buy clothing because you love it, not because you feel you *need* a whole new wardrobe. Buy with intention, and buy piece by piece so that you can grow into your wardrobe. Start to have fun with mixing and matching different things. Try wearing the pieces you do have, slightly differently. Do you always wear baggier shirts? Try tucking them in one day and see how that feels. Do you wear dresses? Try adding a belt to it today. That kind of thing. Play with it and be curious! You might even surprise yourself.

An Extra Dose of Magic
A few things to ask as you look in your closet and drawers:
- Do you love your clothes?
- Do you feel confident in them?
- Do you use them to hide behind?
- What do you feel when you put on different clothes from your closet?
- Do you like the feeling of the fabric?
- Are your clothes outdated or has your style changed as you've changed? Start to ask yourself why you wear what you wear.

If you are feeling completely lost, there are mavens you can seek out here too! There are shopping services available that will come and look at your closet, and help you go through to create outfits with what you have. There are also services that will offer a colour analysis to see what colours suit your skin tone. There are body analyses to look at your body shape to show you what styles suit your body type best. There are mavens that will even go shopping with you, teaching you to shop and assist you in store to see what works for you and what doesn't.

This is something as women especially, that can be overwhelming. We feel like we should know how to dress and how to shop, but were you ever taught? I sure wasn't. I went with my mum or friends, and I *witnessed* them shop. But I was never taught *how to* shop. It was all trial and error, and believe me, I am constantly learning as I evolve. If hiring a service doesn't feel right, try asking a friend – someone who you often think of as knowing what they're doing, or someone whose outfits you always compliment! More than likely, they would be honoured that you think that highly of them to ask for their support. Be honest with them and tell them you love their outfits, and you are thinking it is time to update your wardrobe. Would they be interested in going shopping with you, teaching you any tricks they might know and helping you to find some new items?

Connecting to Your Body:

It's easy to start to run on autopilot, missing the cues our body is telling us; to slow down, tune in, or speed up. Not only does this include, physical health and wellbeing, but our intuition and our innate wisdom that the body carries. So, before we go any further, take a deep breath in. Feel that air move through you, filling you up with a lightness, and as you exhale, allow the breath to move out of you. Simply noticing your breath. Use your hands to take a moment and feel your body. Run them up and down your legs and your opposite arms, just saying "hey body, thank you for being here". Notice what areas of your body feel tight, do you need to stretch something? Is it time to adjust, and sit in a different position? Pay attention to these simple cues and start to bring awareness back into your body. You will start to connect to your physical being. Noticing your physical body is an important step in seeing yourself again and in remembering who you are here to be.

Seeing Your Body:

There are various levels of this, I encourage you to start wherever you're comfortable and move through each step as slowly as you need to. Mirror Work is about looking at yourself in the mirror. It is about spending time with yourself and with whatever emotions comes up. Each time you approach the mirror, set the intention of seeing yourself fully, for all that you are – for the beautiful being that you are. We are approaching ourselves through the lens of observation, simply to see. Not to judge, not to criticize, not to fix or to change. Simply to see.

Find a moment or create time, where you are home alone, or have a moment to yourself where you can lock the door. You're welcome to do this with others around, but from personal experience, removing the self-conscious fear of someone possibly seeing what you're doing, makes it way more comfortable as you get started!

The first thing you can do, is look at yourself in the mirror, fully dressed. A full-body mirror preferably. Look yourself up and down and take note. Take note of your body posture, and of how you hold yourself. Can you sit up or stand a little taller? Can you pull your shoulders back? Start to move your body – slowly, while watching yourself move in the mirror. Become aware of how you move. Look behind you, from the side, try to see as many angles as you can. Try looking at yourself standing, then sitting. Perhaps dancing, swaying side to side, or jumping up and down. Simply move and admire your body as you go, witnessing your body as it moves. Notice if you're making eye contact with yourself, or if you're focused on a particular area of your body.

Simply observe.

How does it feel to see yourself? How does it feel to look at yourself? Take note of what is coming up for you – are you emotional? Are you self-conscious? Shy? Empowered? Surprised at what you see?

If this feels uncomfortable at first, you can ease into it more gently, by sitting in front of the mirror and journaling what you see. It allows you to take purposeful breaks from looking at yourself, while still allowing you to process the emotions that you are feeling.

If this feels comfortable, the next step is to take off a layer of clothing, preferably in your bra and underwear or activewear. Repeating the method above and simply observing your body. Noticing how you move, how different parts of your body fold and bend, or jiggle and bounce. Noticing the dimples of your skin, the colouring of your veins, freckles or scars. Taking extra time to be curious. Where does your hair grow? What direction does it grow in? Explore your body and get to know your physical being.

The next layer is to remove all of your clothing. In the nude, start to do the same thing. Observing your body with curiosity, noticing how you move unrestricted by clothing.

Find something about your body that you love each time, something positive to focus on. If negative self-talk or an unfriendly comment starts to creep its way in, try seeing that comment from love. Those stretch marks that you don't necessarily love – thank them for growing with you. Thank your body for allowing it to adapt as it needed to. That scar that bothers you – why do you have it? What lesson did it teach you and how can you find gratitude for it?

I broke my ankle a few years ago and now one ankle has a lot of scarring and is noticeably bigger than the other one due to the extra metal plates and screws. I don't love the physical scar, but I love what it taught me. Breaking my ankle forced me to slow down and re-evaluate my career. This was at a time in my life while I was working a job that wasn't the right fit for me. My employer and I were not on the same page, and if I'm honest, I'm pretty sure I was going to be let go the day I fell. I slipped on black ice in the parking lot and because of that I was covered under Workplace Insurance and compensated for six months while I recovered. Had the break not happened at work I would have spent my time healing stressing about where my next paycheque was coming from, with the focus of needing to get back to work. Breaking my ankle at work, gave me time. Time to think about what I really wanted, and how I really was. There were many little lessons within this experience, but the biggest one was that I wasn't happy working for someone else – I wanted to start my own business. I don't love the scars but I have so much gratitude for them, that I am able to see them with love now.

An Extra Dose of Magic

Also, notice my wording – at the time, I referred to this as an accident, but over time it became an experience. When we are in the present emotions of something deemed 'negative' we often use negative words, like accident. Now, reflecting on it, I can see the positive in it and I lovingly refer to the same incident as an experience. Notice what words you are using to describe your experiences as you talk about your body. Notice where you are still speaking with a negative undertone, and where you still have work to do to shift your perspective.

If you want to continue exploring your body, physical touch and self-pleasure is a great way to witness your body respond and react. Notice the texture of your skin, feel the warm and cold areas across your body. What happens as you explore? Where do you get goosebumps or do you blush? Does your body automatically move and respond in a certain manner? Were you aware your body responded or felt or looked a certain way? Get super curious and explore! After all this is your body! You should know it best. Continue each step of the way to see your body with so much love and gratitude.

Another tool you can use to further connect and see your body is to do a photoshoot (clothing optional). In October of 2020, I was feeling so disconnected to my physical body. I was deep into learning about energy work, and had neglected my physical body. Constantly with the thought running in the background that I should lose some weight, tone up, *then* I'd feel good in my body. Honestly, I felt like I was living outside of my body and not really giving her any credit for all that she was capable of. I took this feeling and choose to do a photoshoot to help me re-connect to my body.

I often felt a disconnect when I saw photos of myself that other people had taken, so I chose to do this photoshoot to see myself through the eyes of a photographer. It was incredible. I chose my location and photographer very carefully, wanting to work with someone whose work I admired, who I had met already, and knew I'd be comfortable with. Yet someone, I didn't know well enough to make it awkward to be in lingerie! Setting the intention of seeing myself with only love was *key*. I knew these photos were for me and I didn't have to share them with anyone if I didn't want to. I had my hair and makeup done as well, and got a light spray tan to bring some colour into my pale Canadian winter skin. I felt gorgeous! And the confidence shows in the photos. If I were to do it again, I think I would keep it more natural next time, simple makeup, and hair. There's no wrong way to do this though, choose whatever combination is going to make you feel the most confident stepping into that photoshoot.

With the intention of seeing myself through the eyes of a photographer, I was able to look at the photos with curiosity. There were quite a few that I will probably never share publicly, or will strategically crop. But I don't hate any of them. I was able to see, what I would've previously considered a flaw, with an "oh interesting that this happens when I sit like that" perspective. With curiosity and an increased level of self-awareness.

Speaking to Your Body:

How do you speak to your body? How did you speak to your body during the Mirror Work? Did you notice self-criticism coming in, or were you able to speak kindly?

Your body is a beautiful creation. It has gotten you through so many years of life. It has kept you safe, it keeps you nourished and protected. It has the ability to heal, and to grow. You would not be here today without it. Quite literally. Look at how much you have accomplished in this body. For example, if you don't love the cellulite on your legs, think about where those legs have taken you. What rooms have you walked or moved into? What countries have those legs carried you to?

I often used to try to cover my upper arms, but now I look at them with awe. Look at all the people those arms have hugged! Look at the strength that they carry, the art that they have created, etc. Look at where your body has gotten you and speak to it kindly. Compliment and acknowledge all that it does and continues to do for you!

> "You are gorgeous and full of so much knowledge and
> wisdom from all of your years on this Earth.
> You have so much to share with the world.
> Beautiful girl, you deserve to shine!"

> Ruth Montgomery, Journal Entry

Listening to Your Body:

Generally, we are so disconnected from our bodies. We are taught from such a young age to seek external validation first, and to rely on external guidance before trusting ourselves. From day one, when something is off with our body or we are not feeling well, we go to the doctor. When something in our home is broken, we call the carpenter. When our car isn't working, we call the mechanic. These are all are amazing professionals, and I am not discrediting any of them – we need all of these people in our lives and in our network. We are not meant to do all of these things alone, and it is absolutely okay, and frankly encouraged to ask for support. The point I am making is that everywhere we look we are taught to ask someone else *first*. We take their advice and, perhaps if we're bold enough, we ask for a second opinion. However, we generally accept their information as fact because they are the expert and they know best. For a lot of people, the narrative is that these are our experts, they are trained in whatever area therefore they know more than I could know about this topic. I should, and I must, listen to them.

When it comes to your body, you are the expert on it. Only you, can be the maven of your body. You know best. Always. You are the only one who has lived inside it; who lives and breathes it and who knows when something is feeling off or different. You know. Your gut instinct is there for a reason – this is your inner knowing or your intuition. This is your energy centre lighting up in your sacral chakra to say, "Hey, remember me? I have something to tell you!"

When we're feeling disconnected, not only from each other, but from ourselves, we tend to second guess our intuition. The good news is, you can start to remind your body to trust itself again. The not-so-great news is that it may not come as quickly as you'd like, especially if you've been ignoring it for years. In the meantime, the external people and mavens in your life can absolutely offer advice, and insight.

Your intuition is the part of you that just knows something. It's that piece of you that doesn't always have the words to describe it, but with every cell in your body you know. You know that's the right move or the right next step when it feels like a *hell yes!* You know it's going to work out better than you could imagine.

Your intuition also starts to sense the energy in others, without necessarily knowing why you are drawn to a certain person or thing. The more and more you start to build up your trust with yourself, you will start to have a greater awareness of this intuition within you.

This also comes in as our gut instinct – when we know something is off, or unsafe, and can't describe why. When we get that feeling of *nope! This isn't for me.* Trust your intuition – it always knows best. I have learned this the hard way. It has happened twice in my life where upon meeting someone, I immediately had a "nope, I can't be friends with you" feeling. Like something was really off. Both times, I pushed through and formed a relationship with them anyways because logically on paper, they were the nicest, kindest people. My friends liked them, or they happened to like the same thing I did, etc. There are a million reasons my brain could come up with as to why I should give them a chance. Both times, they turned out to be big life lessons in trusting my gut. They both turned out not be who I thought they were, and my intuition had an "I told you so" moment. I have since learned. Always, always, trust your first instincts when it comes to people, or to opportunities. It also works the other way – in saying yes to something that makes absolutely no sense to your brain, but your body is like let's do it! Those always pay off way more than you could imagine.

If your intuition has been trying to communicate with you over the years, and you've continually ignored it; it implies you're saying, 'I'm not sure I trust you'. By asking external experts instead or by doing the complete opposite of what your gut instinct or intuition told you, it re-affirms that lack of trust. Your brain starts to lose trust in your gut instinct and intuition. Creating a disconnect from your mind and your body. And if you've ever lost trust in someone, you know that it is not something you can just wake up and decide to trust them again. It takes practice and repetitive actions, slowly reminding you and proving to yourself that the trust is there.

There are a few simple things you can start to do to build that trust. The first one is in the morning, when you are trying to decide what to wear. Choose the first outfit and stick with it. Something in you said that's what you wanted to wear today. So, wear it. When you try on five different outfits, it creates confusion and the illusion that you trust yourself, but ultimately, you've second-guessed that first instinct.

Another way to start to build trust within yourself is when you are getting something to eat. Easy right? How many times do you open the fridge knowing you're hungry only to pull something out, look at it, put it back, close the door, and come back to it again and repeat the same process 5 minutes later. Are you hungry or not? Something in you told you to go to the fridge. So, if you find yourself in this situation, ask yourself:

'Am I actually hungry?' *Yes.*

'What does my body need?' *(And listen to the first thing that comes to mind).*

'Am I actually hungry?' *No.*

Close the fridge door, and ask 'what do I need instead?' Perhaps it's water, or movement – let your body guide you.

Directions is another great example. A lot of us don't trust ourselves when it comes to directions because we've grown up with digital maps and Global Positioning Systems (GPS) telling us where to go. This can create a disconnect or the feeling of disconnect in "not needing to know" because again, we're relying on something outside of ourselves. Think about the last time you drove somewhere new. When you were driving, did you pay attention to where you were going? Now think about the last time you drove somewhere new and someone else was driving. Did you pay attention to where you were going? Probably not. That feeling of, "someone else has got it" is a similar feeling to relying on a GPS. How many people do you know that have driven a route a hundred times, yet still put in into the GPS "just to be safe"? These little comments and thoughts are little digs at your intuition and gut instinct, saying "I don't fully trust you, so I'm going to put a safety net in place just to be sure!" Ouch. Your poor intuition.

Imagine if a friend constantly made little comments like that to you. We've all had a friend (or parent) like that, or been the friend that does that at some point. Slowly, you start to shut down, and start to think, "why would I share my thoughts or opinions, they're not going to listen anyways?" Slowly, over time, it makes you want to stay quiet. This is what we do constantly to our own intuition when we ignore it.

A perfect way to start to re-program that is to go for a walk, in your hometown, or somewhere you know. Turn your phone or GPS off and put it away. There is no need for music or podcasts in this instance as you want to be fully present and ready to listen to your intuition – distraction free. When you come to a street corner, ask yourself "do I want to go straight, left or right?" And listen. What comes to mind first? This is your intuition speaking to you. Go that way, and when you get to the next street corner, ask again. Slowly with each micro-decision, your intuition is building up confidence, thinking "Oh! You're listening to me!". Trust that it knows what's best, and if you're not "hearing" anything, start to ask, what direction *feels* best.

Our gut instinct is meant to protect us, but when we have shut it down over and over again, we second guess it. When it really matters it becomes hard to determine where that feeling is coming from.

Building this trust back up and re-connecting with our intuition is so important in these small moments. If you trust it in the small moments, you will be able to trust in the bigger moments. For instance, when you're starting to dive deeper into things like your purpose, your passions, where you want to live, who you want as a partner or even medical decisions that are right for your body. This is not to say you won't get lost or make a poor decision again – it just means you're giving yourself the chance to see what your body feels is right for you first. The more you start to trust your intuition, the more you will start to have confidence in your decisions.

Your home and your body are the first steps in re-connecting to your human experience. You are here to be human and fully experience all that it has to offer. However, it's easy to get stuck on autopilot just moving with the flow of people around us. What I have shared in this section are tools that you can come back to time and time again. You can use them to create checkpoints for yourself to make sure everything still resonates with you, or to see where you've veered off path so you can re-direct. Be gentle with yourself through this process and take your time.

Inner Child

Your Inner Child knows where your curiosity is stored. When you were little you could spend hours doing something, with no intention or required outcome; simply because you were enjoying it. Connecting to your inner child is one of the most potent tools you can use. They are the only one, who truly remembers who you were before the world around you told you who you "should" be. It can feel so far removed from your current state, so it's okay if it doesn't all come flooding back. Let your inner child show you slowly what you need to be reminded of.

When we are little, and again when we are nearing death, we are naturally more connected to our souls and the spiritual world. Have you ever noticed a baby looking up in a corner and giggling as if someone is making them laugh? It is believed that they are communicating with loved ones who have past, because they can see the spirit world. We start to come into our humanness as we interact with more humans, and are taught how we *should* behave. A lot of us have learned to disconnect from our spiritual self because the other adults in our lives don't necessarily understand it. Somewhere early on, the narrative around us starts to shift from celebrating ourselves and from simply who we are *being* in this world to what we can do, achieve or accomplish. Accomplishments are valuable, but they shouldn't gauge our worth or importance.

From such a young age, we are taught to look to the future to what we will do. When you were little, you were asked, "what do you want to be when you grow up?" When you were in high school, you were asked, "where do you want to go to school, or what career do you want to have?" When you were in college or university (or figuring out the work force), you were asked, "Where do you see yourself in 5 years?"

We're expected to have it all figured out from such a young age. Yet, in our teens and twenties we barely know who we are because we are trying so hard to morph into the version of us that is liked and celebrated by our peers. The version of us that our parents or role models trust and respect. The version of us that society has deemed "most likely to succeed". But what does that even mean? What does success look like to you? How could you possibly know, when from day one we are taught to look forward and follow the path laid out for us?

It doesn't stop there, either. We are constantly asked "what's next?" This happens with most milestones, but an example that's familiar to most is:

'When will you find the partner to spend the rest of your life with?'

You find the partner and they ask, 'When will you get married?'

You get married and they ask, 'When are you having kids?'

You have your first child and they ask, 'When do you think you'll have the next one?'

You get it. The never-ending hamster wheel of "what's next?" We've all been there; we've all asked and received similar questions. None of these are asked maliciously or intended to stress you out, but why are they so normalized? It can be constant and overwhelming; *always* looking to the future. No wonder so many of us have trouble living in the moment. In the now.

Our Inner Child knows how to live in the moment. It is in their purity and innocence that we remove expectations, and timelines. We can allow them to simply be; to be in and to actually experience the world. To be in their imagination *and* to be in their body. To run and skip – praised for dancing and acting silly. We can join them where their creativity is considered a masterpiece and hung on the fridge for everyone to see. Where they are celebrated for their happiness and laughter with such enthusiasm. When did that stop? When did we start to be measured by what we could "do" instead of celebrated for who we could "be"? We are human beings. Here to *be* in the world. Not human doings. Yet, we live in a world that has taught us success comes from how much you can do. As adults we have to re-teach ourselves this; how to *be* in the world more often.

Connecting with your Inner Child reminds you of the simplicity of being. They can remind you of who you are and how to re-incorporate that back into your life as an adult. Thinking back to your childhood what did you love to do? Re-connecting to that inner joy, and that freedom of childlike bliss helps you to get out of your adult brain of what you "should" be doing today, and reminds your body of the simple joys of life.

We are stuck on the roller coaster of what we *need* to do too often. Whether it's the cycle of getting ready for work or getting the kids ready for school. Working a job that doesn't bring as much fulfillment as it maybe once did, or maybe you've been kidding yourself thinking it will get better. Only to rush home to get to the meeting or sporting event after a quick dinner on the go, just to get home in time to get to bed and do it all over again the next day. On repeat for sometimes 10-30 years.

Have you ever looked at your life and thought, how did I get here? Feeling so far removed from yourself, your dreams, or your pleasures. Our inner child can help us remember who we are, who we came here to be and most importantly how we can find joy.

Who are you? Who were you as a child? Who are you at your core – and are you currently living that? Picture yourself as a child, letting your mind guide you – what age do you picture? Where were you? What were you wearing and how were you feeling?

If nothing immediately comes to mind, picture a certain age. What did you love to play or create at the age of three? Five? Seven? (And every age in between). You can also ask your parents, your siblings, or someone who knew you then to offer insight into your childhood.

Journal Prompts to Connect to Your Inner Child:
1. What did you love doing as a kid?
2. What did you used to spend your time doing?
3. What did you want to be when you grew up?
4. What are you passionate about now?
5. What have you always wanted to try?
6. What does happiness mean to you?
7. What do you love to do?
8. Where in your life can you be more creative?
9. What do you know to be true?
10. If you could go back, what would you tell 7-year-old you?
11. If you could go back, what would you tell 15-year-old you?

Over the last couple of years, we are seeing a shift of people starting to find more passion and purpose in their everyday life. People are starting to find more joy in what they are filling their days with. If you are feeling out of balance, a simple place to start is to bring in elements that your Inner Child loved. Did you love to dance? Take a 3-minute break and have a dance party! Did you love to draw? Find some pencil crayons or markers and play – see what you can create. Was there a class that you used to love? Can you sign up for an adult class or start with a drop-in class and see how it feels?

The other part of our Inner Child, when it comes to play, is the things we missed out on as a child. Maybe your parents couldn't afford to put you in dance classes or sign you up for summer camp – either due to time or financial obligations. Maybe there was something the other kids in your class got to do, that you always wished you could, but felt left out of. You're the adult now, you have full control of your life. Consider this your permission slip to sign up for that class you have always wanted to take, or try that activity or sport you feel like you missed out on. You have the ability and full permission. If time or finances is hindering you right now, ask yourself, 'is it really? Or is that just an excuse I've been telling myself?' Look at the costs and time associated with the thing you really want to do, and break it down.

- What would it actually take to do this?
- How much time each week would I need?
- How much money?
- How can I shift my current schedule to make this happen?
- Why am I finding excuses not to? Am I scared? Nervous? Afraid of what people will think?

Maybe it's not something that can happen overnight, but this can be something to work towards. Set it as a goal for the near future and start to create a plan to make it possible.

If you're still coming up with excuses, it's time to get real with your Inner Child. What are those excuses serving? What deeper story are you holding onto that that narrative plays into? Ask your Inner Child. Picture yourself as a child sitting across from you and ask them, 'why are we holding on to this excuse or this story? Where does it come from and are we ready to let go of it?'

Notice, what comes up for you here. Is it fear? Maybe it is worthiness? Simply observe and ask. Journaling is a great tool for this as well, to start to explore what stories you are holding onto that maybe aren't yours to hold anymore.

"Don't be so concerned with holding onto who you were, that you miss out on who you get to be."

Ruth Montgomery, November 2022 Journal Entry

Recently, I faced a fear with a story I had built up and held on tightly for the last twenty years. The story was that I don't golf, that

I am not a golfer and I am not good at golf. Phew. This was a big one for me. I played in a golf tournament when I was 12 years old, with people much older than me and I was terrible. I could barely hit the ball, and when I did, it was in the wrong direction or barely moved at all compared to the other golfers. Thank goodness it was a Best Ball tournament (where all players on your team play off the best hit each hole), or I would have been there for days. I also have a vague memory of not being good at Tee-Ball as a younger child – both sports requiring good hand-eye coordination. However, I did play a lot of sports growing up – I figure skated, danced, played soccer, basketball, and volleyball. But when it came to golf and baseball, I held on tightly to the belief that I couldn't play those sports. Over the years, I had friends or partners ask me to join them golfing and I turned it down every time, coming up with any excuse. The reality was I was terrified of not being good enough, of being a failure or of drawing attention to myself in a negative way.

In the summer of 2021, I took a leap and I took golf lessons. I contacted a female golf pro in my area that I had followed on Instagram and asked for lessons. She offered me a group session to start – Introduction to Golf with 6 other women. Immediately, I felt uncomfortable and I had to get very real with myself. I knew I would most likely find an excuse not to show up to these group lessons for fear of being seen. I knew this. So, I asked what other options there were and told her how nervous I was. We decided to do three private lessons instead. One was not enough to re-program the fear, and four felt like too many in case I didn't love it. I feared I would start to dread going, again re-installing a dislike for golf. It's a fine line between proving a point to yourself, and over-committing to a point where the plan backfires. After my first session with my golf teacher, I was ecstatic. I did alright for my first time, but truly, just getting out there and facing the fear was the biggest release of a story that no longer served me. A story I had held onto for twenty years took an hour lesson in a supportive environment to dissolve. Honestly, the hardest part was making the initial contact and asking her for help. Admitting that I was terrified, *and* that I was ready. I probably will not go on to play golf regularly, but now if someone asks me, I won't be scared to say yes – and that feels like such a relief.

An Extra Dose of Magic

I learned years ago that excitement and nervousness physically are very similar reactions in the body. It's simply whether we label them as positive or negative emotions. Any time I'm nervous I like to try to trick my brain into telling myself, "I'm feeling these butterflies because I am just SO freaking excited". It almost always works.

The point of sharing this is, sometimes we do need support outside of ourselves, to remind our inner child that it's safe. When connecting to your inner child, if something difficult is coming to the surface, or you feel a reluctance to go within, remind your inner child that they are safe in this moment. You've got them and are protecting them. If it feels bigger than you can or desire to handle alone, hire the mavens that can support you, or ask the friends that can guide you. It's okay to admit that you don't know what you're doing, *and* that you want help. You do not have to do any of this life alone – you are supported more than you know!

An Extra Dose of Magic

If you are feeling alone in this, or are needing extra support, know that it's okay to look outside of your immediate circle if you feel like you don't have the support you need or desire. If you don't have supportive or positive-minded parents, family, friends or co-workers, it's okay to start to look for new or different groups of people. For more ideas on how to do this, *see* **Finding Community** *on page 68.*

If you'd like to further dive into inner child work, you can work with different practitioners and modalities like psycho or somatic therapy practices, meditation, journaling or guided inner child sessions to connect with and heal through any stories that are coming up for you. Please do not do this alone until you feel ready and resourced. Let someone support you until then. Visit *www.themavenproject.ca/bamresources* for more support.

As you re-connect and grow more into yourself you may find your identity starts to shift. It's okay to allow yourself to evolve. What once served you, doesn't need to continue serving you if it feels like you've outgrown it or evolved beyond it.

This evolution can be hard, especially if it's around a job title or an identity we've held onto for years because too often we introduce ourselves with our job title. For instance, "Hi, I'm Ruth Montgomery, I'm an Interior Designer." I studied interior design in college and university and worked in jobs off and on for 10 years as a designer. When I shifted into the world of entrepreneurship and coaching, I felt like I was losing part of myself and part of my identity. We put so much pressure on that title that we work so hard for. And it's the first, and often only subtext when we introduce ourselves. *Wait, what?* I am so much more than a designer, *and* it will always remain a part of me. It is simply a piece of who I am – it solely, does not define me. Just as your title does not define you. I have been drawing my dream homes, complete with secret passages, since I was a child, that wonder and curiosity isn't going anywhere simply because I changed my job title.

An Extra Dose of Magic

Learning to interchange the word "but" with "and" has been a huge shift for me in recognizing that we can have and be multiple things at once. The word "but" iterates that I cannot have both, it is one or the other, or one with the consequences of the other. "And" honours all versions. I can be both an Interior Designer *and* a coach. I can be silly and carefree like a child *and* have the maturity of the adult I want to be. Notice where you use the word "but" and see how it feels to interchange it with the word "and".

There is a transition when you start to lean into more soul-fulfilling work. It's not always easy. It takes looking at yourself from a new perspective and re-learning and unlearning pieces of yourself and your story. It's an important part to re-connecting with yourself, for yourself. Let your Inner Child show you the way back! Let them remind you of all that you are and of the maven you have always been.

"Some of the best experiences happen when we get lost
for a moment and find our way back to ourselves."

Ruth Montgomery, Journal Entry

Spiritual & Energetic Being

"There comes a time when the mind takes a
higher plane of knowledge but can never
prove how it got there."

Albert Einstein

Through diving into personal development work from a spiritual lens,
we start to recognize that there's more. More than us and more than
our human experience. This is where the understanding of a belief, of
God, of The Universe, of Source or a power higher than us comes into
play and the idea that we are all, somehow, interconnected. The
individuals that make up this lifetime are interwoven into other
lifetimes, and will continue to weave in and out of the tapestry of life
for years beyond our human existence.

We are a soul, here to experience a human existence. We are here
to learn, to grow and to heal. By seeing things from this wider
perspective, it allows us to step away from our humanness and see that
everything is happening for us, not to us.

As humans, we experience a lot of emotions and we often deflect
into playing the victim. We tend to take on the mentality that things
are happening to us. We often think that we have been dealt a bad

hand, or that luck had something to do with it. When we can step back and see ourselves, outside of our human existence, as the soul that we are, it is less about us. It becomes about the lesson and the pattern that we are shown and the healing that gets to be done (if we choose).

Our human body is the piece that connects us to each other initially. It is the piece that we can visibly see and it gives us something tangible to understand. Our human mind *needs* that physical piece of comprehension and experience.

Our soul, is the internal piece of us that we cannot see, and the words to describe it vary around the world. Our soul is the part of us that trusts that everything is going to work out better than we can imagine. It is the piece of us nudging ourselves to step further into our purpose by following our passions. Our soul is the piece of us that knows our magic *is* our being.

There are lessons in everything, and when we start to see ourselves as a spiritual being, we can start to remove the ego, and see things outside of ourselves. (*If these terms feel new – we'll get into them more on page 80).*

There are stages of awareness to your spiritual and energetic being and the simplest way to begin to connect to your soul is through silence. It's not necessarily the easiest when we've been so disconnected from ourselves, but it is the best place to begin to create awareness and connect to your spiritual being.

It is so simple to tune out our inner voice, when we don't give it the chance to speak. Tapping into our inner voice doesn't need to look a certain way. It can start with 30 seconds or 30 minutes. You can even set a timer. You can start with 30 seconds of silence, then move to one minute, then two, then five. Let yourself *be*, sitting comfortably, with no distractions, and just start to get comfortable with hearing yourself think. Get to know yourself – start to hear your thoughts in the silence, because you are a pretty incredible human being, and you are worth getting to know.

If that feels difficult, start to disguise that silent time as going for a walk. Giving your body a purpose, will give your spiritual being time to start to find a balance within your body. Leave your phone at home and get outside. Listen to the trees and the birds, feeling the warmth of the sun on you. Take time to notice: how the leaves move, how the grass or dirt feels on your feet, and the sounds around you as you walk. Pausing for a moment, to be in nature. Listening.

You can also simply stand outside, with your feet in the ground. This is called Grounding. Allowing your body to connect with the energy of Mother Earth, helping you to find a calmness. Feel the sand between your toes, taking a deep breath in, reminding your body of just how connected you are – to yourself and to the world around you. And how beautiful life can be in the stillness of it all. You have everything you need within you, and access to the support of being held up by Mother Earth whenever you desire.

You can also begin the next time you go for a drive by turning off the radio and drive in silence. See where your thoughts go. That's all, it's that simple. It's in those pauses, that you'll start to hear yourself. You'll start to see how interconnected with the world and with nature we are. You'll start to understand you are *never* in this alone. There is always an energy around us, supporting us, and guiding us if we listen.

You will start to hear your thoughts, and then eventually, you will start to see your thoughts as they are happening. Like an unbiased witness as you start to understand how your human brain works, and the energetic connection through it all. You'll start to witness where your mind goes, and see the journey it took to get there. You'll start to recognize that every person you meet has the ability to teach you something new. Every interaction has the power to be meaningful and that it's all so beautifully woven in to the tapestry of your story. The world, and the moments start to become filled with awe-inspiring magic.

Meeting your spiritual being is all part of going through a Spiritual Awakening or becoming Spiritually Aware.

An awakening or being awakened, to me, in its simplest form, is being aware of yourself and how you are a part of the bigger picture. As a human, or someone who is "asleep" we often have tunnel vision for our life, and think we are in this alone. As someone who is "awake" we start to see that it is about so much more than just us.

"A Spiritual Awakening is a returning to self."

Ruth Montgomery

A Spiritual Awakening can feel overwhelming and daunting, because what really is it? Through my experience, I believe the process feels a lot like learning a new language in a different country.

Imagine travelling abroad. First, you become aware that there is a language other than your native tongue. You recognize that the people there speak differently than you do.

Second, you start to hear these new words and you try to learn some of the basics. For instance, if you were traveling, these would be the key phrases that you would need such as: please, thank you, and where is the toilet? When exploring this new language, you often start by memorizing them. Then trying to understand how to pronounce them and when to use them.

Third, we start to listen and absorb new words, over and over. As you are immersed in this new language words start to have meaning; you start to recognize those words, and what they mean to you. You start to pick up certain words when you overhear different conversations, or when ordering in a restaurant you start to understand what different things mean by observing the actions or items that follow the words.

Next, comes a deeper understanding. For instance, when you overhear a conversation and you get the gist of what is being said. Or when you start to see words (on menus or street signs) and you know what they mean in your native language.

Then, you try to speak the new language, using small words at first, exploring how the people speaking this language respond to you. Do they understand you? Are you making sense? Slowly pieces come together creating sentences. One sentence at a time, you become more and more confident in your ability to communicate – both by speaking and expressing yourself, and by listening and absorbing what the other person is saying.

Where the magic truly happens, is when you start to think in the new language. You start to process your thoughts in your head in the second language before you speak them. You start to be aware that you aren't translating in your head anymore, you are naturally thinking in the new language, formulating thoughts and speaking those thoughts into the world.

And finally, when they say you truly understand a new language, is when you start dreaming in that new language. When all levels of your being start to understand it. That's the point where they say you are fluent.

Becoming A Maven: A Spiritual Awakening Journey Guide
By Ruth Montgomery

Level of Awakening	Learning A New Language	A Spiritual Awakening Journey
1st	Awareness Of A New Language, Different From Your Own	Awareness Of Your Spiritual Being & Human Body
2nd	Learning The Basic Words (Please, Thank You, Toilet, etc.)	Learning The Basic Terms (Soul vs. Ego, etc.)
3rd	Listening & Absorbing The New Language	Reading Books, Listening To Speakers, Podcasts, Etc.
4th	Starting To Understand	Starting To Feel The Shift Of Self-Awareness
5th	Starting To Speak & Have Conversations	Starting To Find People That Can Communicate With You & Exploring This Through Healing Modalities & Mentors

6th	Processing Thought In The New Language	Embodying This New Language, Self-Reflection
7th	Dreaming In The New Language	Out Of Body Awareness & Seeing Your Thoughts

Like learning anything new, going through a spiritual awakening can be exhausting and uncomfortable. There is a period where you feel completely overwhelmed and possibly like you'll never understand. You may feel like you want to hide, because you don't know which way is up. It's important to take in as much or as little as you desire to, and to give yourself grace as you start to learn this new subject area. It's okay to take time by yourself, for yourself, as you integrate these new understandings. It's like learning any new skill, you're not meant to get it perfectly right off the start.

We learn so much through our mistakes and pre-conceived failures. It's okay to misunderstand and to get things wrong as you grow. And most importantly, it's okay to change your mind as you learn new information. You will fall in love with different tools, lessons and modalities. You may want everyone around you to be as excited about is as you are – it's important to remember here, that just because you are excited about it, doesn't mean everyone around you will be excited about it too. And that's okay. You will start to see who you can share your excitement with, and when you need to explore things on your own. Try not to take it personally – we are each on our own journey.

It's hard not to share when you're learning something new that you are passionate about, or that's changing how you see the world. As you learn more, you may come to understand that what you once thought to be true, doesn't feel important anymore. You may find a new modality that makes more sense to where you are today, or a new way of looking at things that resonates more deeply than it did before.

It is okay to change your mind and it is okay to make mistakes – it is all a part of the journey. Finding a balance between your humanness and your spiritual being is a part of this. Learning to live in, and love both parts of yourself is a unique balance for each of us.

It's also important to remember that each person's journey is their own. There is no timeline for this level of understanding. Some people in your life may never even be open to the first stage of a spiritual awakening journey. There will most definitely be people in your life that think you are slightly crazy, and they may tell you so. And trust me, you will feel crazy at times as you go through this. I pinky promise you; you are not.

> "I thought perhaps she was crazy,
> but she was only highly intuitive."
>
> Carl Jung

Just in case you didn't hear me: you. are. not. crazy.

You are learning something new, something that was once foreign. You are opening yourself up to a whole new world. A new understanding. A new perspective. Once you start to see into this world of a spiritual awakening, it's hard to stop. But know, if it gets difficult, or feels overwhelming, it is absolutely okay to pause for as long as you need to. Trust that the lessons and the people you need will come into your life when you are ready. This is not something you need to rush. This is a lifelong learning and unlearning, and it's all part of the joys of being human.

> "I am writing this from the beach in Santa Monica near the pier.
> Listening to the waves and the after waves. The part where the
> water recedes to become a wave again. That's where I feel I am
> in life at the moment. Retreating to figure out what's next."
>
> Ruth Montgomery, November 2018 Journal Entry

Throughout this journey there are so many emotions that will come up as you start to see things more clearly and through a new lens. Know that whatever you're feeling is okay; your feelings are valid – whatever they are. Our emotions are here to help us process our experiences. It can sometimes feel like a roller coaster – just remember throughout this book, whatever comes up for you is valid and encouraged. Emotional Intelligence is having an awareness of your emotions and recognizing that you are not your emotions. It also brings an awareness with it that you must feel your emotions in order to learn and move through them.

Crying is the easiest way for the body to release what is no longer serving you. Please, throughout this journey, give yourself permission to cry and to feel everything you are feeling. With no judgement or embarrassment. And for the love of all things, do not apologize for crying!

"I'm exhausted from feeling like I'm too much and not enough all at the same time...so, I'm just going to be me. The rest will fall into place."

Ruth Montgomery, August 2020 Journal Entry

If at any point in this book, something doesn't feel right for you, that's okay. Take what resonates and leave the rest. Some teachings or ideas will light up your soul, and others may not be your truth. That's okay. This is your journey. It gets to look like whatever you choose. Notice though when something feels like it's not for you, versus when something feels uncomfortable because you've been living so differently. Uncomfortable can be a good feeling of expansion. It pushes us out of our comfort zone to explore a new possibility.

And if it is a hell no, then that's it. No gets to be an answer as well. No justification needed.

After the final stage of becoming fluent, it can start to feel unfamiliar to speak your original language. Once you've been exposed to this new way of speaking and thinking, it can be hard to adjust between the two. If you've ever watched a child who is learning to speak two languages at once, they mix up their languages in the same sentence. This is often what it feels like.

"I feel out of place.
I worry I appear like I think I'm better than,
but truth is I'm lost. Lost between levels.
Lost as I evolve out of who I once was and
as I'm searching for who I am becoming.
I haven't found the next evolution yet...
I can't even pretend to know who I am becoming...
I don't know what my future holds,
all I know is that if I continue to show up
authentically – I will continue to follow my truth."

Ruth Montgomery, Journal Entry

Throughout this journey, it is so incredibly important to find people who are experiencing this journey and awakening as well. (If you're feeling alone, *see **Finding Community** on page 68.)* As you grow, and evolve, some people may not understand you anymore. You may find that you don't enjoy hanging out with the people that you used to spend the majority of your time with – or at least not as often. It can feel like we are speaking different languages, and it doesn't mean one is better than the other, simply different. *(For more explanation on this, see **Energy & Vibrations** on page 87.)*

Much like learning something new, I love collecting experiences and creating a deeper understanding of self. This brings me so much joy, however, it's bittersweet. Each experience has the power to shift or elevate you further away from your comfort zone. Including the people there.

"Understand that healing and growing can distance you
from people who you once had a bond with, and it can
also bring you closer to those who will heal and grow
with you. The time in between can be difficult
but there is so much to learn in solitude."

Jay Shetty

The highs and lows of a Spiritual Awakening are very real. From one moment, feeling on top of the world, to the next of feeling like what is the point? It can be mentally exhausting. Remember that you are learning something new. And overwhelm comes just before bliss shows up. Don't give up. We need your unique light in this world.

Each level may happen at different speeds as well, and some can be quite overwhelming. On the hard days, treat yourself like a pet or a child. Get out of bed to pee, drink some water, and eat something. There were many dark days throughout seasons of heartache, grief or expansion where my miniature pig, Sophie, was a blessing – reminding me that if I could get out of bed to look after her, I could do those very things for myself. It's important to nourish both our spiritual being, as well as our human body – both are important in order for the other to function fully.

There are moments where it feels overwhelming, and I honestly have had moments where I felt like perhaps something is wrong with me, journaling "it's crazy. I feel crazy. But I know I'm not. I'm able to move through things so rapidly now." When we enter new levels, it can feel like we're spiraling out of control. In these moments, it's okay to pause or slow down, and let your mind and body catch up to your soul.

"What was the spiraling about?"
Reminding you, that you're human.
Here to have human emotions.

"A lot of times I think it would be easier to re-cluse.
Not talk or have human interactions.
I fear I say the wrong thing constantly, or judge."
That's part of what you're here to learn.
The days you speak out of turn are the days you
haven't connected to self.

Ruth Montgomery, March 2021 Journal Entry
– Conversation with my Higher Self

In July of 2019 a friend and I hiked Machu Picchu, completing the 4-day hike on The Inca Trail. Before we started the hike, we had to arrive 2 days prior to acclimatize to the altitude. We had to prepare our bodies, physically for the trail. Each day while we were hiking, we climbed higher in altitude than where we slept each day. We went up to acclimatize our bodies for a moment, and returned to a lower elevation to sleep. The next day we would pass that first elevation and climb even higher, all to go back to a slightly lower altitude to sleep – each day gaining more and more in elevation. This is similar to the journey of a spiritual awakening. When things feel like they are spiraling out of control, we've gone too far, too fast. We have to return to a previous level in order to fully absorb everything. This journey is not a straightforward path, and each is unique. Remember to see each level or moment of this journey with gratitude and love.

"There is a level of self-awareness where you can sit,
separate from your thoughts and simply observe.
This level of enlightenment is possible for us all."

Ruth Montgomery, June 2021 Journal Entry

When you get to the final level of a spiritual awakening, the level of dreaming in the new language, you can start to observe your thoughts. I especially find this, in the stillness of nature. You can see your thoughts arrive, you can watch where and how they connect to the next thought you have. You can see how they travel, and how they go from one spot to the next. You get to witness the change.

Remember the game telephone as a child? Where you'd sit in a circle and one person would whisper a sentence in the ear of the child next to them, and each person would whisper it around the circle until it got back to the first? It was never the same sentence, each time altering slightly, until it had a completely different meaning. This is kind of like observing your thoughts. Previously, you could witness the first thought, and then all of a sudden you were on a tangent and somewhere completely different. At this stage of awareness, it's as if you are observing the game of telephone, hearing how it changes each time it passes from person to person. You can sit back in awe, amazed at how the mind went from one place to the next!

I think it's important to note here that we can go through many spiritual awakenings over time, and throughout our lives. Just as we can learn many different languages, we can experience this process with different lessons and elements of our awakenings. They also can happen simultaneously. While you maybe be at level five with one lesson, you may just be entering level two of a different lesson. This is a constant evolution, if we choose. Sometimes, it may not feel like you have a choice in learning the lesson, but you always have a choice to pause when you need. To take time for yourself, to nourish your body, or rest your mind.

Self-care, and self-compassion are important to remember throughout this journey. If it feels tough, or exhausting, know that there is always a contraction before an expansion. Like an arrow must be pulled backwards before the it can fly forward on the bow. The expansion is coming, and it will get easier – and, in the expansion, when you can look back, you will be so proud of all that learned.

An Extra Dose of Magic
Wherever you are on your journey you matter. And YOU are needed in this world. You are worthy of being seen, respected and most importantly loved. You will always be enough. Never forget that.

PHASE TWO

EXPLORATION

*"Thank you, Universe, for allowing me to live the life I lead.
Thank you for giving me the opportunities, the lessons,
and the dreams I have had thus far, and for all of
the curiosities still to come."*

Ruth Montgomery, A Letter of Thanks

You only know what you know. A lesson taught to me by one of my first business coaches back when I was starting my career as an independent Interior Designer and trying to figure out my place in the world. From a young age I knew I wanted more – I have always sought out opportunities; collecting experiences as I go.

This idea of "you only know what you know" explained so much to me. Let me paint you a picture, in the realm of information available to us, a fraction of that is what you know you know. The next portion is of the information that you are aware of, and you know you don't know it, but you know it's there. For instance, I am aware that there are rocket scientists and I know I do not know the information that they know.

The third portion of information is what you don't know you know. This is the information that comes so easily to us, we don't even recognize it as something we know, it is just a part of us. That information that we assume everyone else has as well. A big lesson in this for me was from a different business mentor who said, you should charge the most for what comes easiest. Just because it comes easiest to us, doesn't mean that it comes easiest to everyone else. This is the sweet spot of where our skills are – in the information that we don't even realize we have. For example, when I was first starting out as a Professional Organizer, I struggled with what to charge people because I thought, 'this is easy, I feel bad asking people to pay for this service'. Not realizing that this was not naturally easy to a lot of people. It was a unique skill that I had or information that I didn't know I knew.

The fourth piece of this pie makes up the majority of it, in the section of what you don't know you don't know. This is the information that we aren't even aware of that exists in the world.

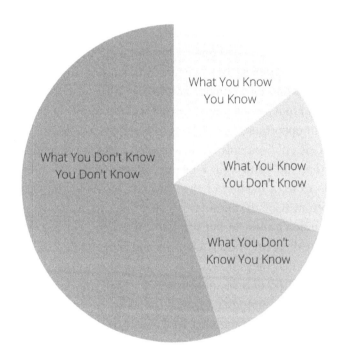

YOU ONLY KNOW **WHAT YOU KNOW**

What this reminds us of is that there is always more to know. We will never know everything, and just when you think you know it all, you don't. Therefore, everything I am writing here is my interpretation based on the knowledge that I currently have. As my knowledge grows and expands, my opinions and beliefs may change. As I encourage you to expand your awareness, I will do the same.

This also means everyone you ever meet knows something you don't. Every interaction has the opportunity to teach you something. Whether it's new information, a new way of looking at things, or seeing things from a different light. Everyone brings with them a different upbringing, a different set of learned experiences, a different set of family values, of work ethic, of cultural and religious backgrounds. As we go out into the world, we add to that repertoire of learned experiences constantly. Every day.

Think about your day, what have you learned today? Or what have you tried that was different than yesterday? We are constantly exploring and interacting with the world around us. Through what we witness, where we physically are, the movies and information we consume, the education and skills we learn. As well as through the conversations not only that we are a part of, but the ones we over-hear. We witness how people respond, and we see how different people express themselves. All little tidbits that somewhere in our brain gets tucked away for later.

When you start to see how different we are, and how much we can learn from each other, you can also start to see how similar we all are. We just come with different back stories. We are all seeking connection and commonality. We are all seeking to be loved, to be seen for who we are, to be heard and to be respected for what we believe in. In fact, we are more alike, than we are different.

It's through exploration that we learn the other elements of what we don't know. It's through exploration of our ideas, of our passions and of our relationships that offer insight into what's waiting for us just beneath the surface!

Lessons In Human Connection

"You don't have a soul. You are a soul.
You have a body."

C.S. Lewis

You are here to experience and explore all that it is to be human. One of the greatest lessons in our human experience is in relation to others. In connecting to other souls having the human experience.

Too often our human interactions remain surface level – beautiful weather we're having today, isn't it? Nothing drives me crazier than a statement like this, especially with a loved one. And yet, still in this, we are searching for commonality. Searching to find that the other person is also witnessing this beautiful weather. When everything else is unknown, or too hard to share, there is a basic connection in things like the weather. We typically will talk about how work is, how the family is or the façade of what's going on in the world. We will ask how are you, without really waiting to hear the answer. We will ask what are you up to or working on these days, without wanting to really go into the details. All of this feels like a game, and sometimes, it's easier to play the game and keep things surface level; especially when you are in the midst of discovering or re-discovering yourself.

Finding those connections where you can go beneath the surface and dive into the depths of your emotions or awareness are a special kind of magic. They can feel sparse, especially when you are looking for them everywhere and desperate to find them.

Sometimes, it's being stuck in the same routine, with the same people that makes it feel surface level. And sometimes, we have to take a hard look at ourselves. When we aren't finding those deeper connections, what can show up is a lack of self-awareness or self-created guards surrounding ourself, blocking us from letting someone else truly see us. Even though we are desperate to find a true connection, we have to ask ourselves, are we showing up fully, in these moments of conversation? Are we truly open to being seen? Are we ready to fully see someone else? This is where the power of vulnerability comes in.

Vulnerability

When we are able share from a place of vulnerability, we give others permission to share vulnerably as well.

> "Vulnerability is the essence of connection,
> and connection is the essence of existence."
>
> Leo Christopher

Vulnerability is hard. It is something we have not been taught to show (especially in business). As an entrepreneur when I was offering Interior Design services, I felt like I was pulled between two realities. One, that I needed to appear successful for people to trust and work with me. Two, that I needed to be open and vulnerable to attract my ideal client. When I was starting, I didn't always know what I was doing as a new entrepreneur. It was hard to ask for support out of fear of appearing unprofessional or unsuccessful – afraid I'd discredit myself to my clients. On the other side of things, we are taught that customers buy from people they trust, and when they feel a connection. So, how do you create connection? Through honesty and vulnerability. Try to figure that one out.

There are two sides to every coin, but this one had my head spinning. As an entrepreneur I felt very alone, not wanting to share this confusion for fear of being 'weak' or 'incapable'. It's very lonely starting out with anything new – be that personal development, entrepreneurship or spiritual development.

I desperately needed community. I needed to know I was not alone in this. I started attending personal development conferences, I hired coaches, and eventually I created what I was searching for in my business The Maven Project and hosted workshops. I asked the speakers to share their stories from a place of vulnerability so that we could start to see ourselves in each other, in the hardships and the successes. To start to share that we were more alike than we were different and that that was worth celebrating.

In sharing from a place of vulnerability, imagine how much further ahead we would be, how many trials and tribulations we would save ourselves from, simply from knowing that others were experiencing similar things. How many hours do we spend trying to solve a problem that our friends have already solved? How many hours do we spend up at night, nervous to share a thought or an idea?

By sharing ourselves from a point of vulnerability, we instantly give others permission to share. They see us letting our guard down, and recognize that it is a safe and sacred place to be open to who they really are and what they are feeling.

Our lives may look different on the outside, but we can relate to the feelings expressed. Through our own stories we can start to normalize what the other person is going through. You'd be amazed at how many instances you think that you've experienced alone, when in reality others have felt they've been in similar situations. All of us, individually, choosing not to share out of fear, yet we are all experiencing different variations of the same thoughts, emotions and insecurities.

Getting to this point of confidence in your vulnerability is the hard part. We assume people will judge us, and criticize us. But the truth is, if they are talking about us and judging us, it's because they've made up their own stories based on their perception of us. We each see the world through the lens of our experiences. How we see other people is more of a reflection of ourselves, than it is of them. So, if our worst fear, is that we will be judged – they're doing it anyways, and it has nothing to do with us. We might as well break free from this narrative, and stop hiding our magic.

This place of seeing ourselves vulnerably allows us to believe in ourselves. And when we believe in ourselves, we can chase the life we truly desire. We can start to unravel the layers of ourselves that we've built up, and the images that we present to the world.

"Many of us have worn our masks for so long that we're not even sure what's actually underneath anymore."

Lewis Howes, The Mask of Masculinity

When we hide ourselves, we give off mixed signals of what we really want. To the Universe and to the people in our lives. We start to feel out of alignment, and unsure of where to go next.

It takes a lot of courage to open up and share your story. It's scary. But you know what's even scarier? Thinking you are in this alone; thinking that you are the only one going through what you're going through. When it's hard lessons, it sucks feeling like you're alone. Society has taught us that it's embarrassing, and we need to put on a brave face. The truth is, vulnerability isn't a negative. It doesn't make you less than.

When we keep things to ourselves, we can also start to normalize behaviours that are not normal. We silently think, either I'm the only one experiencing this, or everyone must be experiencing this – this is just how it is. So many of us have had similar experiences that we have normalized. For example, one year at Camp Maven (our women's only adult summer camp) we had a pelvic floor therapist speak. Initially, a lot of the women didn't think they had any interest in attending her talk. I talked to a lot of the attendees throughout the weekend, asking: Have you had kids? Do you pee when you laugh? Most of them responding with 'well of course'. I shared that this should not be the norm. As women, our bodies can reverse things like this with the proper guidance from someone who can teach us how, like a pelvic floor therapist. When it came time for the talk, approximately 75% of the women showed up and listened. It was the most attended session. This is a topic that is so personal, we rarely talk about it. We casually make reference to it in passing comments trying to make light of an uncomfortable reality for a large majority. Yet it is one of the many topics that is not normal (or doesn't need to be normal) that we collectively, have normalized. What else have we normalized in our day to day, that we have no idea because we're too afraid to look different? We are creatures of conversation and we are meant to talk and to share.

> "We are hardwired for connection. From our mirror
> neurons to language, we are a social species.
> In the absence of authentic connection, we suffer."

> Brené Brown, Dare to Lead

If you're still struggling with being vulnerable, ask yourself: Why am I so afraid to show the world who I am? Your authentic self will be more appreciated and respected. People can sense the insecurity, and feel guarded. They will also feel an inauthenticity, which can sometimes feel like the person is untrustworthy. When someone is out of alignment, we can mirror that energy and feel that something is "off" with them. If we are meeting someone new and trying to create a deep connection, that "off" can show up as friction. Meaning, someone you meet may be out of alignment, but what you feel is that you can't trust them, or you don't resonate with them. It feels icky, like maybe you don't like them. This could be the opposite of the truth, but in a brief encounter with someone who is out of alignment, it can sometimes feel like that. All of this to say, maybe now isn't the time for that connection to flourish. It's okay if you feel like something about that person draws you in, and you meet up with them again in the future. Relationships shouldn't need to be forced, and if your body is screaming at you "I don't like this person" then trust that instinct. Knowing that if you are capable of feeling this way when you meet someone new, they are also capable of feeling that way about you when you first meet. Ultimately, it all comes back to being true to yourself.

"Do you ever feel like you said something you shouldn't have? Do you over-analyze the next day feeling guilty and very aware of where you went wrong? I feel like I don't know how to connect some days. Yet what I seek most is connection."

Ruth Montgomery, September 2019 Journal Entry

We can also shy away from vulnerability after experiencing what I call a "Vulnerability Hangover" (similar to an emotional hangover). That's right, just like if you consumed too much alcohol and are feeling terrible the next day. This can happen when we are vulnerable as well. Especially with someone new, or when we are just starting to explore vulnerability more freely. It's that feeling of, 'oh no! did I share too much? What do they think of me today? I shouldn't have said that'.

All valid, although generally unnecessary. First of all, what feels extremely vulnerable to you, may mean hardly anything to the person you shared with. I know this sounds harsh, but chances are they are busy thinking about what they overshared. What feels heavy, and is hard to share, *is* heavy and hard to share because it affects *you*, not them.

Secondly, this can be an indication, of where your comfort level is. Stepping outside our comfort zone is scary. This is a great gauge for how far to go next time. Perhaps smaller steps next time would be more appropriate. Or if it felt good in the moment, perhaps you're overthinking this because you have entered a new depth with this person and that unknown is also scary – incredible, but scary nonetheless. Your intuition will start to guide you to the right people that feel safe to be vulnerable with. People that will hold sacred space for you as you start to share more from the depths of your heart.

Finding Community

Trying to find your place in this world can be a lonely feat. Finding an authentic community – means you need to show up authentically and with vulnerability.

This journey can be hard to express to other people, and can bring up feelings of shame or guilt. Speaking from experience, we often make the issue bigger in our mind than it actually is. Having someone or a group to share it with can help you to work through that. They will bring you a different perspective which will often allow you to process the memory and move on.

Soul-searching can also be extremely liberating. It's such a powerful thing to feel like you have found your place in the world, and your purpose for being here. It's empowering and exhilarating! However, one of the downfalls is that sometimes we outgrow our friend group. If they are not doing the work on themselves, they may not be able to relate to you all of the time anymore. And that's okay, but by staying in a group like that all of the time *you will get stuck.* There will be a point where you may stop growing in order to still "fit in" with them.

It's important to seek other people and create new friendships that will help foster your growth. I don't agree with totally cutting people out just because they're not on the same level as you yet, but you can limit your time with them so that you can continue to grow without the friendship feeling strained or like a burden to either of you.

Having a community of like-minded people is so important as you're searching for your place in the world. They will encourage you when you are feeling down, and remind you of how amazing you are and that what you're doing in this world is meaningful. They will also tell you how ridiculous you're being when you're overthinking things and need to get out of your own way.

An Extra Dose of Magic

If you feel like you haven't found that community yet, here are a few ways to try meeting new people:

- Attend an event – even solo! Attending events with a friend is great, but it's easy to stay within your duo as you meet people. Attending solo, although scary at first, is liberating, and will push you out of your comfort zone to talk to new people.
- Join a local sports team or committee. There are plenty of options from volunteer organizations, to adult sports teams, to gyms or town event committees, check in with your local recreation department to see what's available or who you should contact.
- Get a part time job or join a Network Marketing Company. It's an easy way to meet new co-workers, or if you're working in retail or restaurants to meet new people in the public. It may not be a job you love long term, but it's a great way to bring in some extra cash flow while meeting people.
- Go online - there are plenty of social media groups that are engaging, and full of like-minded people. Try to find one that's relatively local to you to allow for in-person meet-ups!
- Join a mastermind – a group of like-minded people all working towards a similar goal through a sacred container of growth.

Being Supported

A mentor of mine, Jennie, once asked me to imagine myself as an award-winning actress, winning the Oscar for Best Leading Role in the Award-Winning Feature Film. She reminded me that in order to do this, you must also have Best Supporting Actors and Actresses in your film. These people are crucial to your success. Some of them may come and go, some may walk with you through the entire film and others may show up for a pivotal scene and leave. Some may also show up in the form of the villain, leading you, the main character, to a crucial realization in the plot.

Now imagine that movie, is your life. People come and go. Some stay for a season, or for a lifetime, and some show up just to trigger us, and teach us something. When you can put a lens of cinema on it, it all starts to look a little more eloquent, and little more magical. As we start to remember, this is all happening for me, not to me. These people are all here to support me, as I walk this journey.

Equally, sometimes you will play the Supporting Actress or Actor in someone else's Feature Film. You may show up for a moment, or for a lifetime. You may even appear as the villain. Not that this justifies any terrible things that you've done, but it allows you to step back and see it differently. Have you ever replayed comments that you've made (that maybe felt out of character) or did something you regret? Maybe you had to do that as the supporting role for someone else. Not always of course, but perhaps it was all part of the show.

You may also experience a moment, that doesn't really make sense to your story. Sometimes there are lessons, that feel big, but also feel like they have no relevance to your story. Sometimes, you simply have to play the part of being there so that the main actress or actor can learn a lesson. We can overanalyze every detail of our lives, and it can be easy to slip into victim mode, asking "why me?" Step back and start to look at those moments, as what did you learn? And can you see what the other people learned? The lesson isn't necessarily directly for you.

> "Lighthouses don't go running all over an island looking
> for boats to save; they just stand there shining."

> Anne Lamont

Additionally, sometimes people need to learn a lesson all on their own. So, when we try to swoop in before it's our scene, we actually rob them of the lesson they needed. Be a lighthouse. Let them come to you, when it's time.

We also need to remember that each person is doing the best that they can, with the information that they have. Most people are kind and generous human beings full of love. They are doing the best they can, and that's all we can ask. We need to honour their journey, and honour where they are at in their story.

Everyone else has their own story. This journey is about reclaiming your identity for you and your soul's purpose. If you are overly concerned with everyone else's journey, you will never fulfill your own. As you are on your way to fulfilling your journey and soul purpose, naturally you will help others along the way. If you are focused on your own journey, you will be helping them more than you realize just by being you.

It is not your responsibility to make sure everyone else is okay. Granted if you are a parent or caregiver, you are responsible for feeding your child and keeping them safe until they are old enough to help themselves. With adult relationships though, it is no one's responsibility, nor anyone's business to look after another adult. In fact, sometimes we try to help so much that we are actually debilitating a person and slowing down their lessons because they haven't been able to work through it on their own. We can guide and offer advice when asked, but ultimately, we are each born with the capacity to survive and to thrive. We can continue to nurture and offer support without taking responsibility for the people in our lives. Each of us will take a different path to get to where we need to be to fulfill our destiny and to write our stories.

Perception and Perspective

Perception is everything. Our perception influences who we are and how we carry ourselves. It shapes what we believe to be true about the world around us, what we expect and what we believe about ourselves.

Our perception of the world around us is coming from our lens and our personal life experiences. We can't possibly know all that is happening and how others are thinking, feeling or what they are perceiving. To each person, their perception of what is happening in their lives is about them and how it affects them. As we become more self-aware, we can start to differentiate and find a healthy balance between people-pleasing (where we often neglect our needs for someone else's) and being selfish (where we completely disregard what the other person is going through). Especially as we dive deeper into this work, this becomes so important to find the unique balance for each situation.

It's also important to note that how we see ourselves is often different than how the world sees us. We are our own worst critics, so we will judge and criticize ourselves more than anyone else. Often the people around us are so busy looking at their own "flaws" that they don't notice ours. We spend so much time in our own heads worried about what other people think. We are all worried about what other people think and if we will be accepted. Everyone simply wants to be accepted and seen for who they are. Truth is, we are all so busy thinking about what the other person is thinking about us, that none of us are actually thinking about the other person at all.

We put on these masks and personas to fit what we think other people will expect of us in order to be accepted or to be perceived how we want to be perceived. The truth is, the more spiritually awakened you become, the more you will be able to see through these masks. And the more you will crave to be surrounded by genuine people that have taken their masks off.

The more you step into who you really are, flaws and all, you will be accepted on a far greater scale. When you start surrounding yourself with people that are at this point as well, you will worry less about what they think, and will honour yourself for who you are in a very loving 'take it or leave it' kind of way.

It takes practice and it takes time. It is not always an easy path to get to a point of self-awareness that is so accepting of yourself; it can sometimes feel like one step forward, and two steps back. Even on the days when you truly think you've mastered it, you will have moments where someone does judge you for your flaws or calls you out on something that you are working on.

"Everyone has a story you will never know or understand. What it meant to them, how they've internalized and how it affects them. They might not even know. Be kind."

Ruth Montgomery

The reminder here is that we never know what other people are going through. Every person has so many chapters. You can never possibly know the details of why they act the way they act. Of the things they are guarding themselves from trying to prevent from happening again.

One of your best days, may look like someone else's worst day – you still deserve to celebrate your best day! In the same way that your bad day, may look like someone's better day, but in your world, it's still a bad day. And you get to feel that. The point is, regardless of how your day, your situation, or your emotions compare to someone else's is irrelevant. It is how you perceive it, in the awareness of your own life's experiences.

We can have sympathy for other people, yet until we've experienced something similar, we cannot empathize. Part of the human condition, and what you signed up for was to feel the pain of being alive. Because without the pain, and the perception of what pain means, you would not be able to appreciate and celebrate the joys in your life.

Each person is walking their own story, with their own parameters of what pain, and equally, joy mean to them. To be human from a spiritual lens, is to respect that. Even if you don't understand it.

"It's all about me for me. It's all about them for them.
At the end of the day, that's how we're all walking
Through this life. It's not always about you – sometimes
you need to be in someone else's life to be a lesson."

Ruth Montgomery, April 2020 Journal Entry

As we start to become more self-aware, we start to become more aware of our surroundings, and the people in our lives. We can start to step back naturally, detach and observe the situation through an external lens.

When we are younger, our instinct is to react to each situation. *How does this affect me?* When we are confronted by something uncomfortable, there's this sense of urgency that we have to react right away - sometimes without thought. It can feel messy and rushed, and we often react defensively.

When we can take a pause to see the situation from a different perspective. By not taking the situation as an attack on ourselves or our character we give ourselves the chance to respond. In order to respond, it's important to take pause. This is a great reminder of just how different everyone's perspectives are – how wildly different we perceive the same things or situations.

We start to be able to respond to a situation or statement instead of react. Our natural instinct becomes observe, pause, reflect and then respond. We can ask ourselves, why did this cause a reaction in me? This allows us to start to see things from a wider perspective, playing less of a victim and not always making it all about us.

We can start to shift our perspective on situations and see it from the other side. How might someone else be seeing this? If I were to step back, how would I perceive what is happening? If I were not involved, how would this look? How might the other person be feeling? What might they be experiencing? What might have led them to react the way they did? Does it actually have anything to do with me?

This can be hard. This can mean stepping back physically and emotionally from the situation. When asked for marriage advice on their 35 plus year marriage, the best advice my parents offered was to take 24 hours to respond when you are in a fight. If you get into an argument, acknowledge it, be clear that you are taking time for yourself to respond and wait. That time gives you the space to calm down. It gives your emotions time to settle so you avoid reacting in the heat of the moment, saying something hurtful that you may regret, or that may be irrevocable. When you give that space, you can come back with more perspective on the situation, and with less hurt emotions to calmly discuss the issue at hand. This allows both parties to offer their view of the situation, and the other person is more likely to actively listen. When we react, we often are so busy wanting to make a point, we listen with the intent of responding, and formulate our response while they are still talking. When we respond, we can actively listen, and really hear what the other person is trying to communicate. Then we can take that information, along with our own, and respond in a more authentic manner.

Brené Brown, often talks about using the phrase, "The story I am telling myself is...". This helps to diffuse the situation by clearly stating where our mind went, and by removing the blame from the other person, it gives them a chance to respond calmly. This statement places all responsibility on ourselves. When we can take full responsibility for where our mind has taken us, and what our perception is, we can create lasting solutions.

Judgement

Judgement comes from a place of insecurity, and lack mindset (a mindset that primarily believes in limited opportunities, rather than an abundance mindset which believes abundance is everywhere). When we find ourself placing judgement, it is a great indication of where we still have work to do. Use this as a magnifying glass of where you need to look within your own life.

"The root cause of all judgement is the fear of
not being good enough, not being worthy
of love and not being safe."

Gabrielle Bernstein

These triggers often come up to shine light on our shadows, to show us where a pain point is, that we need to acknowledge. Why are you judging someone else for those words or actions? Is this coming from a place of jealousy or fear? Or out of a lack mindset because you secretly want what they have? There is no need to judge your judgements, we all have them. Simply seeing them for what they are, and asking them why they are there will help you to get to the root of the judgement. Once you can see the root, you can start to see where it really comes from, or where there is still work to be done.

Owning Your Story

This is your story. I think it's important to remember to honour your journey for all that it is. The good, the bad and the not so beautiful.

"In order to love who you are, you cannot
hate the experiences that shaped you."

Andrea Dykstra

The mistakes that we've made, or the frustrating or heartbreaking things that have happened to us, have all shaped us into who we are today. These are not moments to look down upon, but to reflect on the lessons they taught us, allowing us to become who we are today. As Oprah says, "*What happened to you? Not what's wrong with you. Everyone has a moment that would break your heart. What's really going on?*"

There is also a harsh reality of realizing that you are the only person responsible for your story. You are the one in control of writing the storyline. If you are not where you want to be in your story yet, where do you take responsibility for where you are? Yes, there may be external factors, and I am not discrediting any of those. What I am asking, is for you to focus on what is within your control and start there.

When I first started attending personal development conferences, so many of the speakers had such tragic stories. They had succeeded from nothing, had gone through heartache or experienced a tragedy that pulled at your heartstrings. I had moments of doubt in my own story. Who am I to speak? My story isn't nearly as tragic as theirs, I couldn't possibly inspire someone on stage. It took me years to learn that your story doesn't have to be tragic to be worth telling.

Your story is important. It could be the catalyst for someone else's life to change. It could be the inspiration someone needs to go after their dreams. It could be the courage that someone needs to see, to allow themselves to show up in the world, fully owning their story. Don't be afraid to show the world who you are, we need you – all of you.

"Reminder to Self:
You don't have to have it all figured out.
There is magic in that."

Ruth Montgomery

Spiritual Development

There are so many concepts when you're first learning something that it feels like a constant translation is necessary. Treat this section like a reference portion of this book, and if something doesn't make sense right now, know that you can come back to it later. Remember, we are evolving constantly, and lessons come in different orders for each of us. Trust your journey and know that it is happening exactly as it's meant to; in the opportunities, the lessons *and* the timing of it all. This section is my current understanding of it all. Yours may be different, and that's okay. We can use those differences to learn from each other – that's part of what makes this experience so beautiful. In saying that, take what resonates, and leave the rest. This is your journey!

A **Spiritual Awakening** refers to a shift in consciousness. It is a returning of self and it is a returning to self. Learning to trust yourself, your intuition, and what your body is telling you. Learning to trust internal validation as much, if not, more than, external sources. Consciousness refers to our state of awareness. What we know and could share. Subconsciousness refers to the programming that we are unaware of, but that operates and impacts how we behave and what we understand.

An Extra Dose of Magic

Returning of Self: This can feel like you are remembering parts of yourself, long forgotten. Little habits, thoughts or 'knowings' (things you knew but couldn't explain why you knew them) that you've had over the years that have never made sense, but you've known they were true. This can feel like those pieces of yourself are starting to make sense, fit together and fall into alignment.

Returning to Self: This can feel like you are returning to a previous version of yourself. One that you've forgotten or gotten away from over the years. If you've ever woke up thinking, 'how did I get here?' in a sense of this is not what you expected from your life, or if you've ever felt 'I don't know who I am anymore' – a spiritual awakening can feel like a returning to self. It can feel like finding your way back to yourself, or a version of you that you truly feel connected to.

Spiritual Awareness refers to the recognition that there is more than just our human existence. Recognition of a greater source such as Spirit, God, Source or The Universe.

Enlightenment refers to seeing things more clearly from a wider lens – seeing how things interact and affect each other in the big picture. Recognizing that each action has consequences or connections, and each piece of who you are has ties to other pieces of your life. Being enlightened, to me, means understanding that everything is connected on a very deep and intrinsic level, physically and energetically.

Your **Inner Knowing** is your soul energy. It is your essence and your truth. It is who you are at your heart centre and who you are as a spiritual being.

Remembering often happens throughout a spiritual awakening. This is where when you learn something and it doesn't feel like new information, although logically it is new to you in this lifetime. As an example, this happened for me when I first learned Reiki *(a form of energy work – for more info see page 93)*. I thought for sure Reiki would be the piece I felt I was missing – it would be *the* piece I needed to find what I was supposed to do. Soon after my mentor started working with reiki with me, I knew what to do, without knowing consciously what to do. It was this feeling, or this knowing, that I had done this before. Of course, there were still things I needed to learn and be reminded of, but taking the course helped to open up and re-connect me to that knowledge that I already had from previous lifetimes *(see page 134 information on Past Lives)* as a healer.

Soul vs. Ego

As mentioned before, you are a soul having a human experience. Your **soul** is the piece of you that just knows. It is the essence of who you are and all that you are here to learn and expand on in this lifetime.

Your **ego** is the part of you that is here to protect you. The part of you that is human and knows what is safe. Psychologically and physically, our bodies are programmed to keep us alive. Their sole mission is survival. When the body feels attacked, we have a fight, flight or freeze response. The fight response is meant to put up a fight and stand up for what you believe in, or know to be true. The flight response is to run and hide and get as far away from the danger as quickly as possible. The freeze response is the piece of us that stops us in our tracks and freezes, the part that plays dead, hoping the danger will pass.

The ego is the part of us that remembers when our fear was heightened and our survival was jeopardized. Our ego can also be fairly dramatic in this day and age. When it senses any hint of fear, our ego often reverts to that old behaviour that previously kept us 'safe'. It is the part of us that keeps us in a relationship or a job, that on some level we *know* isn't serving us anymore, but our human brain and our ego justify staying because it's familiar. Our soul is the part of us that knows there is something better.

The ego fights with the practicalities of a situation, like where are you going to live, how will you eat, where is your next paycheque coming from? The ego is terrified of change and can only see what it knows. So, staying where it is familiar is *safer* than branching out into the unknown.

The soul is the part that says, I don't know, but I trust that it will all work out. The soul is excited by evolution, and growth. It wants to push our limits, to see what we're capable of, because it knows that we are capable of incredible things! Your soul craves change and expansion – your soul wants you to become the best and biggest version you can be.

It's like having the devil and the angel on each shoulder, one pushing you to try something new, and one pushing you to stay safe. Depending on the situation, you can decide which is which. I like to think of the soul as the rebel inside of us that is full of confidence! The ego inside of us, wants to stay small so that we don't disrupt things.

"Don't dim your light to make others feel comfortable.
Shine your light, so they know what's possible."

Unknown

This quote is the perfect example of our ego vs. our soul. Our ego wants to feel safe and stay small. Our soul knows we have a light and purpose worth shining so all the world can see it. Both have their time and place, and our ego absolutely serves a purpose. If there's hesitation when you are stepping into something new or slightly uncomfortable, be sure to check in with yourself. Is this coming from my soul or my ego?

When it's coming from our ego, and we're stepping more into our soul, fear will often show up. This can look like: fear of success, fear of failure, fear of being seen, and/or imposter syndrome. Impostor syndrome for example, is the feeling of, 'who am I to be doing this work or speaking on this topic?'

When fear shows up, ask yourself if you are physically in immediate danger. Is there anything around you that could harm you? If the answer is no, then the fear only exists if we give it the power to. When fear shows up it is a very loud indication that you are nearing the edge of your comfort zone and your ego is trying to pull you back. When this fear shows up, courage is created. The more you expand, the more courage you create, and the braver you get. Do what scares you because this is where the magic lies! Fear only exists when we give it meaning, and purpose to exist. If we shift our perspective and see it as the creation of courage, we can do anything!

An Extra Dose of Magic
When your ego shows up trying to protect you, ask yourself:
1. Am I in any immediate danger?
2. Is this fear true?
3. Is this fear or belief still serving me?
a. If yes, okay, thank you. What do I still need to learn from this?
b. If no, Is it safe to release this?

Often by asking these questions, we can rationalize with our ego to recognize that there is nothing to be scared of, and its protection is unnecessary in this moment. If you answer yes to any of those questions, then we can thank our ego for doing its job. This also would be a great time to work further with the support of a coach, Somatics therapy healer or a Reiki practitioner.

As children, we are more in touch with our souls. We haven't been tainted yet by expectations or responsibilities. Our ego hasn't realized how dangerous and hurtful the world and our surroundings can be. When we are children we follow our dreams, and pursue hobbies out of pure passion and joy, because we don't know any better. We haven't learned yet, that we "should" follow a societal standard.

As we get older, our ego's voice gets louder and louder, and it starts to overshadow our soul's voice. I picture our ego as the bully in school, that just keeps talking louder and louder until people listen. Not necessarily changing what they are saying – just getting louder. As most of us know, the bully in school, is just a kid who feels unloved searching for love and belonging.

Our soul, I picture as a carefree hippie, with wildflowers in her hair running through the meadow. Carefree and happy to go with the flow. Our soul is in such a blissful state, and just happy to have a human body that it doesn't always recognize that we are listening to it less and less.

We go through a time period where our ego runs the show. We listen to what we should and shouldn't do, we take other people's opinions over our own. And over time, that carefree hippie starts to get restless. Our human body isn't listening anymore, and who once was easy going, starts to see what's happening. Our soul starts to realize that we are getting further and further away from our soul's purpose and it's time to shake things up! It's time to wake us up. She'll start talking to us in the quiet moments – gentle at first, through a flutter of excitement in your stomach, to goosebumps at a new idea on your arms, or a full body chill down your spine of connection. She'll start whispering to us during in the middle of the night, through our dreams, and even sometimes loud enough to wake us up! She'll start to remind you in your daydreams that there's more to your story. There is more you can do in this lifetime.

That is the beginning of a soul awakening. "Coincidences" will start happening and opportunities that seem too magical to be real will start presenting themselves. Our soul starts to connect with our spirit team *(for more info on Spirit Team see page 121)* to align, and offer assistance through mentors, or other humans acting as mirrors. We start to recognize what we don't want, and we question why. Why are you working a job you dislike? Why are you surrounding yourself with people that don't support you? Why aren't you happy anymore? Where is the joy?

An Extra Dose of Magic

Mirrors: People show up as mirrors for us, reflecting what we perhaps can't see because we are too close to ourselves. This can show up as qualities we admire in others, that we wish to develop further in ourselves, or already have, and just can't see them yet. This can also show up in traits we dislike, asking us to recognize where we also have similar behaviours that perhaps we need to re-adjust. This doesn't mean that everyone needs to be used as a mirror, but acknowledging that we have the ability to see those reflections in others, to recognize them within ourselves.

You will start to recognize the energetic vibrations of the people around you and see the similarities in people you aspire to be like, or in the presence of. You will notice as your soul emerges through the fog, that emotionally and energetically some people will no longer understand you.

When we start to open up to our own levels of consciousness (or awareness), and intuition, we can start to see and hear things that we can't explain from our experiences as human. I believe we all have the ability to be psychic *and* it's a practice. Some people will never explore those levels of consciousness, and that's beautiful. Some people will start to open up to that, and not have the words or community to express what they are experiencing and it gets stopped at a certain level. Yet in community, when we start to open up to this level of ourselves, we start to find others that also have the verbiage to explore what we are experiencing. It's normal to hear your intuition, yet we've normalized numbing it with substances like drugs and alcohol, or distractions such as television and music.

People may start to question your sanity. Hearing voices, and whispers can start to feel like you are going crazy – and society may quickly label you as such. "Crazy" is the label given when someone doesn't understand, thereby they remain "normal", and you become "different". It's not a bad thing, but it can feel like it. We are all uniquely different, and when we can embrace those differences, the world becomes a little more magical!

Travelling in Portugal recently, I was amazed at the beautiful tiles throughout the cities. In Cascais, Portugal in particular, most of the tiles in the streets were from the same black and white foundation. Yet from street to street the design and layout was completely different, making them each unique. Each doorway you pass is one of a kind, varying in colour, windows, millwork, ironwork, and landscaping growing up around it. I was amazed at the brightly coloured houses, and how beautiful they were standing in all their glory.

What was even more fascinating though, than how those beautiful, bold houses stood out, and grabbed your attention - was how they made you notice the simple, clean, white houses. If it had been a row of white houses, they would have all blended together, and you probably wouldn't have really noticed any of them. But because a few brave houses, took the chance of being bold, it allowed the other, more basic houses to stand out in their simplicity.

Your journey will be unique, and your mental health throughout this lifetime is so important. Whatever you are feeling or experiencing, although it may be confusing, it is valid. Your feelings are valid *and* your thoughts and emotions are important. Don't let someone who doesn't understand belittle or negate what you are going through. Find someone that does understand, or that has the tools to help you understand.

> "In a world with too many labels,
> I hope you remember they don't define you."

> Ruth Montgomery

When we step into something that is unknown, it is easier to place a label on it than to explore what's really going on. We are quick to find a label to explain the symptoms of something, rather than do the work to find where the root of those symptoms are coming from. This goes for a lot of things, especially from a more Western Medicine approach. Not always, but more often than not – we want a quick solution so we can get back to our busy lives. Digging in, and discovering the root of things is not a quick solution. It takes time, and energy, and with each level it can bring with it an unearthing of a whole new layer. This is an unlearning in itself, a different way of doing things for ourselves. For our ego, sometimes we can label it. For our soul, sometimes it is our soul screaming at us to wake up to our potential or to see things from a different perspective. Know that you are not alone in whatever you are experiencing. There are so many people out there that understand and will happily welcome you into their community as you discover this next evolution of yourself.

"The restlessness I feel inside is not because I'm lonely but because my soul feels trapped. It's suffocating. It needs air. It needs to breath."

Ruth Montgomery, December 2019 Journal Entry

I have a theory that at one point in history, a lot of our psychiatric patients could have been hearing messages from source and spirit. They were in a spiritual awakening but when they told people that they were hearing voices they automatically got admitted for medical help because as a society we have labelled them as crazy. Giving them a label is easier for our egos to understand, rather than to acknowledge the soul expansion of others.

Many of us that are experiencing an awakening at this point. Many of us were witches in a past life and were persecuted for sharing our wisdom and magic. There's a part of us, the ego, that is actually trying to protect us from that happening again. I hear it a lot from clients, and I've said it myself, by labeling ourselves as crazy before the other person has the chance. Either, "this may sound crazy, but..." or "I don't mean to sound crazy", etc. I promise you; you are not.

Witches

Witches are also known as Wise Women. Women who were in touch with their intuition, and with Mother Nature. People who created tinctures and healing potions from natural ingredients. Healers who instinctively *knew* what to do because they were in tune with their intuition. They were functioning from a place of alignment, where the soul and the ego worked together – and that is powerful magic. The power of standing in your own being, fully and completely. These women (and men) were persecuted for simply being in tune with themselves, for appearing to have magical powers, because it scared the people around them who did not understand. And instead of trying to understand, the witches were labelled as different, and therefore bad. There are many witches walking this earth today, and chances are if you're reading this, you too were a witch in a past life or two. You have this incredible knowingness within you, it's not something anyone can teach you, it's something you remember. I think we all have that ability within us. To remember who we are.

There are a lot of people dealing with a "witch wound" in this lifetime. In that, in a past life they were literally killed for speaking their truth and sharing their gifts. The ego in this lifetime remembers that, and out of protection, doesn't feel safe to speak up for themselves in this lifetime. We can honour that protection with gratitude and start to look for simple reminders where it is safe to speak your truth in this lifetime.

Let's normalize trusting our intuition. Let's allow ourselves to trust our inner voice, to listen to our intuition and our guides.

You may make mistakes as you are navigating this spiritual awakening, so remember to forgive yourself easily and regularly as you learn and become more aware. You are allowed to make mistakes, and if you reflect on them choosing to learn from them, you are breaking the pattern. You are encouraged to change your mind and to give yourself grace for where you currently are on your journey. Each person's journey is unique and operates on its own timeline. So, take your time, and enjoy this beautiful process!

Energy & Vibrations

We are all made up of energy. We are energetic beings. When energy is emitted, it puts out different levels of vibration. Vibrational energy, is the energy that we emit. Our emotions are what we feel. Yet each emotion has a vibrational level. This is where we often hear about higher and lower vibrations of our emotions, and often relate lower vibrational energy to being negative emotions. The same way we talk about higher vibrational energy being our positive emotions. The truth of emotions, however, is that there is no good or bad. We need to experience all levels of emotion in order to understand and correlate them to each other because without one, we cannot fully understand the others.

EMOTIONAL **VIBRATIONAL ENERGY**

700+	Enlightenment
	Joy
528	Love
	Willingness
200	Courage
	Pride
100	Fear
	Grief
30	Guilt
0	Shame

Vibrational Energy (measured and depicted in hertz)
This was originally discovered and created by author David R. Hawkins
as Levels of Consciousness. If you want to learn more check out
pmore of his work.

This vibrational energy transmits into the energy that we put out into the world, and what we receive back from other people. Simply put, when you feel someone is happy or in love, you want to be near them, you want to experience their energy – it's magnetic. And when someone is sad, we may want to spend less time with them, or need to be away from their energy. It's okay, and extremely important to have lower emotional days and to feel the feelings associated with each level, so honour where you are. But recognize that you have the ability to move through the energy if you are feeling stuck into a different vibrational level. You also have the ability to protect yourself so that someone else's energy, doesn't affect yours. *(For more on how to protect your energy, see page 102).*

Not only do our emotions have an energetic output, but our levels of self-awareness create an energetic output. This energy can also help to explain why sometimes we don't "vibe" well with certain people. It also gives the phrase "not at our level" a different kind of meaning. This is not to be confused with a better or worse scenario, it is simply different levels. We each put off a vibrational energy and throughout our lives we will adapt and grow, and certain things may happen to bring us down.

What's interesting is our attachment to others in this instance. Have you ever felt like you've "outgrown" someone? Or you feel like they are "pulling you down"?

We all vibrate at different levels, and through each stage you will be surrounded by people vibrating at a similar level. This is why, I believe, friendships come and go. People are placed into our lives for a season, with each season varying in length. Either for us to learn something from them, or for them to learn something from us.

Relationships can start to shift if one person is starting to do the work of personal development to try to understand themselves more, and the other person is not. They are content staying within their comfort zone. This can start to put a strain on the relationship as one person starts to raise their vibrational energy. Imagine an elastic band attaching the two people in relationship. If one person is staying still, and the other is moving away through expansion of self-awareness, it creates a tension on the band. Either that band is going to snap, often causing a bit of an explosion as one person continues to soar. Or that band is going to pull the person trying to learn more about themselves back, and to release the tension they will often settle back into or near the comfort zone of the other person. Giving meaning to the term "settling".

You can prevent this from happening, by walking away from the relationship, or cutting the band. Allowing both parties to individually stay or move into the energy that excites them. This doesn't mean forever necessarily. Have you had a friend from say, college or school days, and at the time you were so in sync with how you saw the world, and your goals and aspirations, and then you start to notice as one takes on a new job, or starts to take new courses, or meets new people, you start to drift? Only to come back to each other years later, as if nothing happened, but both more in alignment with who you are? This is because for the moment you were in, you were moving at different paces. Overtime, perhaps one person got to a certain level of awareness and paused. The other person started doing more self-awareness work, at their own pace, and in the first person's pause, this allowed them to "catch-up" so to speak.

This happens with seasons as well. Friendships come and go as we ebb and flow out of different seasons. Each season is different for everyone, but if the relationship is meant to last or is significant, your seasons may align again later. Each seasonal relationship, or relationships at each level of awareness have value. Not more or less, just different value – as you start to flow through levels, if you are feeling lost, try to be present with each level you are in and find something to be grateful for. That simple appreciation helps bring a peace to what can sometimes feel a bit chaotic.

Friends and relationships are our biggest teachers in this life. Sometimes, as hard as it is in the moment, the best thing you can do for yourself, is to walk away to let yourself grow. And to walk away before the elastic band snaps causing irreversible damage.

This can be done from such a place of love, and sometimes a conversation isn't even necessary. A simple awareness of how you feel after spending time with a person. Do you feel drained and exhausted? Or do you feel happy and full of energy? This is your body's way of telling you, from an energetic level whether someone is a good fit for you or not. This can change, it could be based on what they, or yourself, are currently going through. If it's an important relationship, be sure to check in often and communicate what you are experiencing. Make sure it's still leaving you feeling fulfilled!

I have had many friendships where we are growing at different speeds and sometimes, you have to take a break from each other for a few months to grow individually. Often you will find yourselves at the same frequency again later on, and the friendship will be stronger than ever before! Throughout my life I have had to let relationships go because we have grown apart. Some have almost permanently ended, a few have just become less frequent as we take on different adventures in our day to day lives, but most come in ebbs and flows. I have also been let go as a friend when the other person is going through changes that I can't adapt to. This is not a bad thing – it hurts like hell sometimes if we don't understand what is happening. But in the end, when we can take a step back and get some perspective, it's clear to see that it happened for the right reasons.

If you are in a relationship currently, specifically a romantic one, and are starting to tap into your self-awareness (hello, you're here reading this book!) and find your partner just "doesn't get it" – try to take a step back and appreciate that they are in their own journey, on their own timeline. Personal development isn't for everyone, and as you grow, you may feel a strain on the relationship. If the relationship is one of substance, it's worth working for. Try to share with your partner what you're learning from a place of curiosity and excitement. They may see your excitement, and know it's important to you. Start to encourage them to find their own mentors or books so you can share in these together. If they're still not understanding the significance, you can start to listen to podcasts in their presence or suggest documentaries to watch together. As they start to absorb some of the information of growth and personal development it may start to pique their interest to explore more on their own.

Remember, we often resist what we don't know, or what we know to be different. It may take them time, and they may never find the excitement in it for themselves. If this is the case, try to see it from their perspective – what are they excited about, that you are not? And how can you start to be more involved, or excited about their interests? By you taking the time to express more of an interest in what they are learning about, they may naturally start to reciprocate. How can you expect someone to be excited about what you're interested in, if you're not willing to explore what they're interested in?

Cards of Conversations are also a great tool to start to ask deeper questions to get to know each other on a different level. By learning more about each other, it allows the curiosity to continue being explored. And by using a tool like a conversation starter, it allows you to see it as separate. Rather than you drilling them with questions, you are randomly picking a card together to talk about. It feels more curious, and less interrogative.

I like to think that each of us is floating at a different energy level and throughout our lives, that changes. But at each stage in our life, we need to find people at the same level. You'll often hear people talking about "up leveling" and coming into a new level of awareness of who we are and who we want to be. When one person in a relationship starts to explore something new, it can create a fear in the other partner. They may not understand it, or have the words to express it, but they will feel you shifting, and internally fear losing you. I find it's important to share what you are learning and growing through, and if your partner cannot fulfill those needs, or isn't showing an interest, it's important to find a community that can.

This is also a great place to start to look at your expectation management within your relationships. What expectations do you have for certain people in your life? Are they capable of meeting your expectations? Meaning, do they, in their life have the capacity to meet those needs? When you are starting to shift into new levels, be aware of who can meet what expectations for you. Your partner for example, does not need to fill the role of therapist – that's what therapists are for. Be mindful of what expectations you are setting for others, and whether they desire to fill those roles for you or whether you need to find other people to fill those gaps.

When someone doesn't meet your expectations, we can become disappointed. Be honest with yourself, did you ever tell them what your expectations were? Or are they disappointing you or not meeting your level of expectations unknowingly?

This is an interesting cycle, because as a human, we start to place the blame outside of ourselves. Yet as a spiritual being, we can start to see the role we played in the situation. Not to place blame, or guilt, but to create an awareness around ourselves. It's okay to ask for what you want, and to share your expectations with those you are in relationship with, and in turn, ask what they expect from their relationship with you.

A lot of our disappointment, or miscommunication being human happens in mis-management of expectations. As we become more self-aware, we start to expect others to rise up with us. It creates a desire to teach, but it's not always our place to teach. Sometimes, we have to step back and let them learn for themselves. Sometimes by trying to teach, before they're ready, we're actually robbing them of the lesson. Remember you have your own story, and your own timeline.

Energy In Our Bodies: Reiki & Somatics

Our bodies are vessels, and although they can expand and contract physically, our bodies only have so much space within them to hold our emotions. Picture your body as the physical vessel that it is – as the container that holds your energy. Each time we experience something of heightened emotion – positive or negative – it takes up space. Overtime, if we don't process our emotions, our energy gets stuck in our bodies and eventually hits a point of overflow. Past incidents, traumas, and experiences remain in our body, subconsciously affecting our actions, until we release them. It is our body's way of protecting us.

One of the easiest examples is, as a kid imagine being picked on or bullied on the playground. It's embarrassing and hurtful and you want the moment to be over as quickly as possible. The other kids stop teasing you and you go inside from recess. The teacher asks what happened, and you pretend that everything is okay because you don't want to talk about it. You go home and your parents ask how your day was, and you ignore them or pretend that everything was fine. You want to move through your experience as quickly as possible. By not expressing those emotions, they get stuck. Those feelings of embarrassment, of shame, of hurt and sadness – they get stuck in our body and our body remembers them. As we move through different experiences, that emotion builds and builds, until suddenly there is no more space. This can result in angry outbursts, or emotional meltdowns.

As children, we are often taught not to cry, to grow up or hide our emotions. However, crying is the easiest way for the body to release stuck emotions. When we get hurt our natural instinct is to cry and often the adults in our lives tell us it'll be okay, stop crying. They mean well, mostly, but this narrative can be harmful. I even catch myself saying it the odd time still, it is so deeply programmed in most of us – so there is no shame if this is something you've said to the children in your life. Moving forward, I think it's important, as adults we help to show children that crying is okay.

Our bodies also act as a map offering energetic guidance to the root causes of the pain, discomfort and heaviness in our bodies. Our bodies are intelligent beings trying to communicate with us constantly. Often our bodies give us whispers when something is off, and when we don't listen, it can start to physically manifest into symptoms or dis-ease. Louise L. Hay's book *"You Can Heal Your Life"* is an excellent resource to start to understand what different parts of the body are trying to tell you.

We can use practices such as Reiki to tap into this layer of what your body already knows and is trying to express. Reiki is a tool to interpret the map of your body. Reiki Practitioners are attuned to use

Source energy *(For more information on Source energy, see page 128)* to tap into your energy, sometimes calling in your Higher Self and Spirit Guides to offer additional support or guidance. A Reiki session can be done through distance or in-person. When in person, you will usually lie on your back on a massage table and the practitioner will place their hands 1-2 inches above your body to move the energy through your chakras and in your auric field. Your auric field is the energy outside of your body. The Reiki Practitioner will often feel in their bodies where you have stuck energy that needs to be moved out of the body and processed. Some practitioners will be prompted to ask questions to get you to connect to what you are experiencing so you can notice where your mind goes. This doesn't always need to be shared out loud, but noticing what memories surface is an indicator of what needs to be felt or sat with still. Sometimes we have to feel the emotions again to release them. Working with a practitioner can remind the body, that we are not in any harm, that this is a safe space to feel these emotions. We remind our body, that they are not real, we are simply feeling them again in order to release them from our body.

Other times, the mind doesn't need to be reminded of anything, and doing a Reiki session simply gives your body a safe space to release. When doing Reiki, some people will cry, laugh or suddenly take a deep inhale or exhale. All beautiful ways for your body to release what is no longer serving you. When experiencing Reiki people may also feel hot and cold sensations through the body. The practitioner will use the energy to notice where there is work that needs to be done – using the body as a map.

Somatic Therapy works similarly, except that in Reiki, the practitioner is moving the energy for and with you. In Somatic Therapy, the practitioner will guide you asking you to sit with your emotions and where they are showing up in your body. It's almost a combination (very loosely) of talk therapy and energy work. For example, if you are feeling angry about something, the practitioner will ask you to check in with your body to determine where you feel that anger. Once we can acknowledge where that emotion is, we can ask what does it need to tell you? Often this emotion is showing up simply to be validated. Once we bring awareness, the Somatic Practitioner can help to acknowledge, and bring self-awareness to what that emotion is. Often witnessing it, is all the body is wanting. Simply to feel your feelings.

Meditation and physical movement are also great ways to move through the energy.

> "I see the beauty in the depths of my pain. For when you can experience pain, only then can you experience bliss."

Ruth Montgomery, March 2022 Journal Entry

Our pain and our sufferings offer us the awareness to experience joy. Pain will show up in your body when your body is trying to communicate with you. Have you ever experienced pain or disease, that can't seem to be explained by medical professionals? Often, it's because your body is trying to communicate with you on an energetic level.

Things happen for a reason and our body is no different. The body is trying to communicate with you. When there is pain that can't be described from a Western Medicine stand point, it's often because there's something deeper and more energetic going on, something that could be explained from a more Eastern Healing standpoint.

What if we started to go within first, before we sought out external guidance? Start to ask your body what is it trying to tell you – what does it need? Try switching your approach to healing by having that conversation with your body first. Then, if you still need help in understanding what's going on, you can start to explore and seek help from others. A lot of this work is often deeply rooted in patterns and behaviours that we maybe aren't even aware of. Seeking external guidance and support is often necessary. We all need support, and guidance; there is no shame in that. Often these experts, Eastern or

Western focused, have years of experience that they can tap into and offer solutions faster. But listening to ourselves is the first step in truly healing the pain in our body. Opening up that level of communication to the body to say, "I'm here. I'm listening. What do you need?"

Energy can get stuck in our body when we don't process or reflect on an experience or the emotions fully. It can stay in our body until we experience something similar again. A simple example of this is when you stub your toe and become irate. It doesn't make sense why you are so mad, but you are. It was an accident, a simple mistake, and the pain generally subsides relatively quickly. When this happens, I imagine the little green soldiers from the movies *Toy Story*, radioing to their other soldiers saying, 'okay, she's mad, send out as many of the troops as we can while we have the chance. Go, go, go!' It's like our body seizes the opportunity to release as much of that emotion as we can.

It could also play out as a repeated experience. For example, in August of 2011, I was lifeguarding on our local beach on Lake Huron when a tornado came through. Typically, we don't get tornados in my area, and I had never experienced one here. I was lifeguarding on a cold and rainy day with two other lifeguards. We had closed the beach for swimmers because of lightning and were waiting out the storm in our plywood guard hut on the beach. We were watching the storm come across the lake, and all of a sudden it got really dark. We saw a funnel cloud, and joked that it looked like a funnel cloud, but that it couldn't be. The clouds quickly rolled in covering the eye of the storm and the golf ball sized hail started. From start to finish, the storm took less than 20 minutes to come across the lake, and for the skies to clear. We videotaped the whole thing from behind our single pane glass, in our plywood guard hut. Not once did we think we should move to the concrete bathrooms behind us for cover.

We packed up our things after that as the work day was done, and thought we'd go to our local coffee shop to grab hot chocolates before we all headed home because we were cold and wet. We left the guard hut and started driving towards town only to see trees uprooted everywhere. There was an ambulance ahead of us where a person working in a French fry truck at the other end of the beach was being put on a stretcher treated for burns as the fry truck rolled during the storm. We suddenly realized, in the chaos of talking to the other bystanders and paramedics, that we would not be going for hot chocolate. The whole town had lost power, trees were down everywhere, houses were ripped apart, the town was a mess and we had officially just survived a tornado. Fortunately for the three of us, the tornado followed the river into town and missed us. Had it continued coming straight for us, we would most likely have died. We all started trying to call our parents to let them know we were safe, and barely had any cell service. Understanding the panic on the other end of the phone and realizing what we had been oblivious to, set in the reality of what we just experienced. I drove home after that, having to bypass multiple other smaller towns due to the extensiveness of the damage. I got home, safely and spent the next couple of days, in and out of the basement under more tornado warnings.

The Weather Network used our video footage of the storm, because we had been some of the only people to be silly enough to stay and watch it. I made light of it off over the years, as "what an experience!". It wasn't until September of 2021 that I realized how much it had affected me. I was working, this time at a part time job, just packing up for the day (again) when my boss called my co-worker and I to say please stay there, there is a tornado currently going through your hometown. Almost immediately, I started to experience, what I can only describe as a minor panic attack. I called my parents, who were in the basement with my brother and our family dog. I called my sister who was just getting in her car from another town to go home and I immediately told her she needed to go to a friend of mine's house in that town and wait out the storm. I needed to know she was safe, because the thought of her driving home in a tornado brought back a fear I cannot explain. She could hear it in my voice and knew I was serious, even though the sun was shining where she was and it probably seemed completely irrational. We all waited it out, and in that moment, the realization of the severity of the tornado ten years prior sunk in. I was lucky to be alive. Even writing this now, there is still so much emotion attached to this memory, but with each memory of it, more and more releases from my body. I am safe. My family is safe. Our homes are safe. We did experience some damage to our family cottage with this past tornado, and the landscape has changed again with the loss of so many trees. There were a lot of people's cottages and farms damaged but no one was hurt. Everyone stayed safe. It took ten years for me to understand the significance of that event. An event that lasted less than 20 minutes really.

It can be as simple as a comment on the school playground, being excluded from an event you really wanted to be a part of, to something your sibling said as an off-hand comment that they don't even remember. The length of time, or the significance of the event is easy to rationalize to our adult selves. However, we hold onto that energy from whatever age we were at when we experienced that thing. We need to honour those past versions. We need to see the younger versions of ourselves, and remind them that their feelings are valid, that they are safe, and that we've got them.

Energy Chakras

We have energy chakras in our body that also act as a map to show us where there is blocked energy, or where we need support in our day to day lives. Practices like Reiki and Yoga will often tap into these energy sources to understand what is going on. Here is a brief introduction into what each chakra represents, where it is located in the body and what colour is associated with it. If you are doing energy work, and start to see colours, this often indicates which chakra needs attention, or wants to show you something. I have included mantras that you can use to communicate with each chakra to remind them that you are listening.

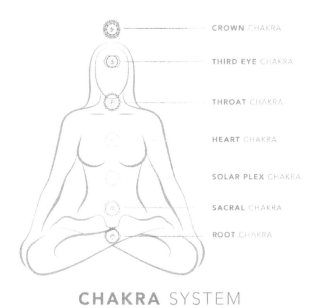

CROWN CHAKRA

THIRD EYE CHAKRA

THROAT CHAKRA

HEART CHAKRA

SOLAR PLEX CHAKRA

SACRAL CHAKRA

ROOT CHAKRA

CHAKRA SYSTEM

The **Root Chakra** is red and it is found at the base of our spine. This represents feeling grounded, safe and secure in your body. "I am safe to be fully myself in this lifetime."

The **Sacral Chakra** is orange and it is found in your womb space as a woman, or just below the belly button. This represents your creative energy and your ability to birth new ideas, or life. "I am a creative being, here to be in creation."

The **Solar Plexus Chakra** is yellow and it is found just below the rib cage. This represents your self-confidence, and the light you radiate to others. I picture it as our own tiny little sunshine within our body. When this is clouded, it's like being on a cloudy day. "I am here to shine my light."

The **Heart Chakra** is green and it is found in your heart space in the centre of your rib cage. This represents your ability to give and receive love. "I am meant to give and receive love in equal abundance."

The **Throat Chakra** is blue and it is found in your throat. This represents your ability to speak your truth and to share your voice. "My voice matters, and my story is important."

The **Third Eye Chakra** is purple and it is found directly between your eyes, in the centre of your skull. This is your ability to connect to your psychic abilities and intuitive nature. "I am a maven and it is safe for me to access my intuitive gifts."

The **Crown Chakra** is white (or gold) and it is found about 2 inches above your head. This is the only chakra outside of your physical body. This is your ability to connect to Source energy and to know that you are always connected. "I am infinitely supported."

When these chakras need attention energetically, we may have physical ailments show up in the organs near or associated with these chakras. Working with a practitioner to start to open up communication with these chakras is one of the best ways, to ensure you are supported as you start to understand your body. Not that you can't do it yourself, but like anything new, when we have someone confirm that we are in fact feeling what we are feeling energetically it speeds up the process to confidently move forward.

Something to consider as well, is if you are having trouble losing weight in a particular area, there is often an energetic block relating to your chakras in that area. Your body is so powerful that it will create a physical barrier to protect its energetic chakra. For example, one of my biggest lessons that comes up over and over again, is opening my heart chakra and allowing unconditional love in. Coincidentally, I developed large breasts from a very young age as if I unintentionally manifested this extra physical barrier to protect my heart. This is not some magic diet, or transformation, but an offering of awareness to look beyond our physical knowing, and go within. As a side note, one of my first energy sessions that I had, I physically lost six pounds. With the healer I was working with, we released so much energy that I had been holding onto I physically felt lighter after, and when I weighed myself the next morning, I was down weight. I didn't visibly see a difference, but I felt it. This is not always the case, and it hasn't happened since, but how amazing is our body to know how to protect us like that? Often after experiencing energy work or reiki, you will feel lighter in your body, as if 'a weight has been lifted.'

We also instinctually protect ourselves when we are in conversation with others. Have you ever noticed, you're sitting, and suddenly realize your hand is on your heart? Or you pull your purse across your lap, for no reason? You will notice with other people too, if something becomes too vulnerable, they may cross their arms over their heart, or turn to face you on an angle instead of fully facing towards you. We shift and adjust our bodies to create an extra barrier, because something in us, puts up a cautionary yellow flag to say, hmm something doesn't feel quite right. Notice what area of your body you are protecting and how it corresponds with what chakra. It works the same when we feel safe, we may start a conversation with our guard up. As we get comfortable with someone, our body recognizes that this is safe, and we may naturally uncross our arms, or turn to face someone with our whole body. Start to notice the cues your body is instinctually telling you.

I've also had it come up a few times with clients, who suddenly feel their heart pounding. They are under no medical distress (and if you are, please seek immediate medical attention) but it feels similar to an anxiety attack. And the message that has come through was, how many people go through life not even knowing they have a heartbeat. How cool is it that yours is giving you life? Sometimes our body just wants to remind us of how connected we are.

Protecting & Calling Back Your Energy

As you start to become aware of your energy, you will start to be aware of others' as well. There are two things to note with this, how to protect your energy and how to call back your energy.

To protect your energy, there are a couple of visualizations I like to use. The one I love most, is calling upon the spiritual guidance of Archangel Michael, the Archangel of Protection *(for more information on Archangels see page 121)*. You can invite him in and ask him to place you in a golden white light bubble of protection. Visualizing a translucent bubble starting from the top of your head wrapping down in front and behind you, closing at your feet. And again, from the top of your head wrapping down on either side of you, fully encasing you in a three-to-six-foot bubble, closing at your feet.

Another one, would be to imagine yourself inside a cozy cabin, with an energetic security guard at the door. Knowing that nothing is able to get through. You could even visualize turning the deadbolts and closing the blinds.

With both methods, you are creating a barrier to protect your energy. You are setting the intention that you are only allowing energy of the highest vibration of love into this safe space, and ask that any lower vibrational energy be alchemized or transformed into the energy of love.

An Extra Dose of Magic

To set the intention to protect your energy, you can say something like this:

"Archangel Michael, I ask you to place me in a golden white light bubble of protection. This bubble will repel any lower vibrational energy from others, and allow that energy to return to where it came from with love. I ask that any lower vibrational energy that may arise within me, be alchemized into the highest vibration of love. Please keep me within this bubble of protection for the next 24 hours. Thank you for your support."

This is a great tool to use when you know you are going to be surrounded by a lot of people or before you are going to be doing energy work. It can also be used if you know you will be visiting with someone who brings your energy down, or is constantly more on the negative side.

Over our lives we create connections with people, and through extended periods of time spent together, through physical, sexual or emotional attachment we create energetic ties, or cords to those people. When we are starting to do this work, we want to start to cut

103

those ties and return that energy to each person. We can cut ties knowing it does not need to cut the love or emotional connection unless we want it to.

Picture yourself standing in the middle of the room, with all of the people you've ever dated standing around you and picture a cord coming out of your body and attaching to theirs. Now add in all of your close friends that you've had over the years. It starts to get messy right? Naturally we will have cut some of those ties without realizing, but some of the bigger attachments, or bigger lessons, hold on a little longer. Cutting those ties is a simple visualization that you can start to release their energy from you, from a place of love. You can work with an energy practitioner using what is often called "Cord Cutting" to do this if it feels heavy or confusing. You can also start to practice this yourself, by visualizing one person at a time whose tie to you is no longer serving you. See them with so much love, and thank them for the energy that you exchanged, and for the lessons that you had. Visualize yourself cutting the tie (with scissors, a knife, or a sword) and sending it back to them. Watching the end attached to you fizzle back into you and imagine yourself filling that hole where the tie once was with a brilliant white light so that they cannot reattach their cord.

If you can't seem to cut the cord, perhaps there's more to that lesson that you need to reflect on. Take some time to journal about your experience and see what comes up. Being honest about your part in it as well, and what you learned.

You can use this practice to release anything that's tethering you to the past that you no longer desire, or that's no longer serving you. Ask yourself, who do I need to forgive? What experiences do I need to forgive? What am I ready to release? Remembering all of this is from a place of love, and that when we start to tap into this energy, we want to do it from a place of deep gratitude and respect.

Masculine & Feminine

We all have masculine and feminine energy within our bodies, regardless of our gender or gender identity. Both are not always equal, nor is one more intense based on your gender. Both have qualities that are incredibly important.

In our masculine energy we tend to show up in hustle mindset, it's focused and logical, full of confidence – often feels more intense or like a more solidified energy. When we are too far in our Masculine, we can show up in what you will sometimes see called the wounded or toxic masculine – this can appear as aggressive or controlling.

In our feminine energy we show up as reflective, open and trusting – it often feels more intuitive, vulnerable and flowy. When we are too far in our Feminine, we can appear manipulative or needy – the wounded or toxic feminine.

Finding the balance between the two, finding *your unique* balance between the two, will allow you to live from a place of authenticity. We need both elements. We need the hard work, dedication, hustle mindset of the masculine as well as the softness, the compassion and the heart mindset of the feminine. We often get stuck between the head and the heart here, trying to fit into societal 'norms'. We try to connect the two sides of ourselves and to find what balances. Getting sucked in too far to one side, is often labelled as toxic, but more than that it can feel like we're not ourselves. It can feel foreign and like we don't know who we are.

The balance is like a pendulum, if you swing too far to one side, when you try to come back to centre, gravity will pull you completely to the other side. It may swing back and forth a few times before it settles back into a state of stillness or ease. When you are feeling out of balance, you can start to bring in elements of the opposite energy into your life.

If you are too in your masculine, a simple option is to try lighting a candle to create soft lighting, or take a hot bubble bath and relax into the stillness.

If you are too in your feminine, try moving your body with weightlifting, a high intensity workout or writing out your to do list and complete a physical task.

Our masculine and feminine energy is represented in our body as well. Your right side of your body is your masculine. Your left side of your body is your feminine. Notice in your body, is there a side of your face or body you like more or less? This may be calling you to pay more attention to one side, or honour both for their imperfections and beauty! Allowing yourself to see both as beautiful, but noticing where your body might be asking for more attention or support. I had a Reiki session recently, and we were doing some deep healing work around generational family ties. When we were connecting to the masculine energy in my family, both eyes watered, but I had tears streaming down only the right side of my face. When we were connecting to the feminine energy in my family, again both eyes watered, but I only had tears streaming down the left side of my face. I'm talking full tears – I was a snotty mess! I'm still amazed constantly by how much our body knows, and in that how much wisdom we have within us that we aren't even aware of!

Thinking about your body, is there a side of your body that you always injure? There can be different interpretations for this. If you often hurt one side of your body – it can be that side of the body calling for help and asking for more attention because something is off.

For instance, as I mentioned previously when I broke my right ankle years ago slipping on black ice at a job that was not in alignment for me. My masculine side was calling for attention to show me that I was out of alignment in my job choice.

Recently, I fell down a flight of stairs and broke my right shoulder – leaving my right arm completely immobile for almost 2 months. This forced paused, allowed me to finish writing this book. I started writing this book outside of Florence, Italy and took a few months to let it process knowing I would finish it when I returned home. Coming home I started getting more into my masculine. I had completely been in my feminine travelling in flow, taking each day as it came, with no real plan. Immediately upon returning home, I was feeling the "need" to start bringing money back in. Clients and social engagements were reaching out and I kept saying yes, over and over until I had filled my time in the masculine hustle mindset. This injury, forced me to pause to continue writing this book. With a shoulder injury, I also had to surrender completely to being taken care of, including having my mum help me shower initially, my sister and friends help to do my hair, and my family to prepare meals for me. It also, from a very literal sense, required my left side (my feminine) to nurture my right side (my masculine). It forced me to find more of a balance.

Both of these instances showed me that I was too far out of balance. The Universe has a sick sense of humour when it comes to this type of stuff, and if you're not listening, it will force you to pay attention.

It's important to remember too that this energy is fluid – there are some situations and moments that will require more or less of each. This is all a part of the beautiful dance of life – we get to be both masculine and feminine. We also get to have it all, and we get to change our mind.

If this section pulls something in you, and you are asking how to move through this energy, there can be some deep-rooted energy or belief patterns to uncover. There are mavens and healers who are experts in these areas, who offer coaching, courses, and energy work – please seek support if this feels overwhelming.

Three-Dimensional & Five-Dimensional

We live in a three-dimensional world – this is where we operate as humans. This is the world of seeing what you believe, of our human existence. This is the physical, tangible world we live in. Where things live and breathe as three dimensional with depth and volume.

In spiritual development you will hear mention of the five-dimensional world. From a very basic standpoint, this is what we know to be true on a spiritual realm. This is where our awakening and awareness becomes outside of ourselves as humans. Where we start to explore our soul and the connections to our spiritual world. You've had glimpses operating in this world since you were a child. If this feels illogical, or you find yourself questioning this, ask yourself where Santa Clause and the Tooth Fairy lived? Make-believe or not, it was a belief you knew to be true as a child without proof of their existence.

Soul Contracts

Your soul is the essence of who you are, living inside your human body. The human body is simply the vehicle for our soul to pursue its purpose in this lifetime. The belief here I want you to explore, is that we chose to enter into this world, for this human experience, at this particular time, and in the bodies that we are in. We chose where in the world we would live, the date we would be born and who our parents would be based on the experiences that our soul needed to have in this lifetime. Your soul chose this body to fulfil its needs for this lifetime. Everything that you love about yourself is here to serve your greatest and highest good, and everything that you dislike about yourself offers something for you to learn to appreciate or find acceptance with.

Before we come to this human experience, we make a plan for what lessons we need to learn this time. It is believed by many mediums I know that we travel in soul families, and often we reincarnate with the same few hundred souls. Each time the relationship could vary. For example, my dad may have been my child in a past life, and my best friend may have been my worst enemy. Part of this, is the idea of soul contracts. We sign contracts with other souls, as an agreement of what we are willing to do to or with another soul so that one or both of us can learn whatever lesson or receive whatever blessing we need for our soul journey.

When it comes to family and specifically parents, we choose them because there is something we need to learn from them. This can either be from the environment we were raised in, or the people that are and the characteristics they offer. If you have negative feelings towards your upbringing, try to shift your focus to recognize that there is a reason you chose that lifestyle. What values did you learn, and what obstacles did you overcome by growing up around the people and places that you did?

At the end of the day, each person is doing the best that they can with what they know. We can't ask any more of them. As author John Gray says, *"Demanding that someone is more than they are is not love."*

For me, I could not be doing what I am doing without a family that is as supportive as mine. They believe in me, even if they don't always understand my ideas. They have given me the space, physically, financially and mentally to be at peace as I continue on this journey working towards my purpose to help other humans re-connect with their souls.

Take a look at where you are today, and what you have done in your lifetime due to your upbringing. Good or bad. What lessons have you learned? Who have you helped along the way? And how can you find or show appreciation for it?

We are often triggered by our parents because we see the traits in them that we dislike about ourselves. It's a great reminder when I am being triggered by something they have said or did, to remind myself, that I, in fact, chose them. I can't change them. I chose them for exactly who they were long before I arrived. Often the people closest to us trigger us the most. They reflect back what we don't want to see in ourselves, so that we are able to see it more clearly. If you find you are being triggered, be sure to give yourself some space – go for a walk, get some fresh air, and take a deep breath. This will allow you, to see the trigger with a clear head, which will allow you to more easily see what it is trying to teach you.

> "If you're around anything enough
> you start to take it for granted."
>
> Tony Robbins

In relationship with significant partners or characters in our lives, there is so much we can learn from these relationships. First of all, to be aware of who you allow into your space and energetic being. Sex, for instance, can be explored as S.E.X. or a sacred energy exchange. Women or the receiving partner literally receive their partner's energy as they physically release. As women, our bodies take on that physical energy, absorbing their energy and are left to alchemize it. Within that energy comes their emotions and their unprocessed traumas. Sex also has the power to create life – just think about that for a moment. The magic of what our bodies and our energy can do when combined!

Energetically and emotionally allowing someone to take up space in your heart is a beautiful and vulnerable experience. An important piece of connection, and when it ends, it can be devastating. Healing through loss and heartbreak, I have learned that the people that hurt us the most in this lifetime, loved us the most in a past life.

> "The soul agreed to hurt you in this lifetime so you could become who you need to become. They loved you so much in a past life to be able to hurt you this time. You signed a life contract."

> Harriette Jackson on Soul Monadic Contracts

This helped me shift any pain and hurt, to a place of gratitude and love. Thank you for loving me so much, that you were willing to sacrifice who you were to me in this lifetime, in order to fulfill the lesson that I needed to learn. What can you learn from your previous relationships? What did they teach you? How can you see them with love?

Friendships or partners come and go, and the levels of intimacy within these friendships will change as you grow. As Lori Harder shares in *A Tribe Called Bliss*, "Part of being self-aware is knowing when someone is no longer meant to be walking in front of you or by your side, and when it's okay to pass them."

Our relationships act like mirrors for us. We see our experiences through our own lens. When you are in an intimate relationship with someone, you gain access to their thoughts and behaviours –

witnessing how another mind sees things. Relationships are one of our greatest teachers, we get to see how other people respond to what we say and do. We witness it reflected back to us in their response or reaction. We recognize, where perhaps we need to take more responsibility for our actions, and for our own becoming. Gala Darling states, "It's a reflection on me but not a reflection of me."

Specifically, when we go through a painful interaction, we can see the reflection, and recognize at the same time that it's up to us what we do with that. We can step back and see both sides. We can continue acting how we've always acted, or adjust accordingly. We can forgive ourselves for our actions and take responsibility for the hurt we may cause or the feelings we may experience. It doesn't make you better than or less than, it's simply a chance for an awareness of self. We can ask ourselves, did someone else cause the pain I am experiencing? Or did I allow it?

When we are triggered by someone else, we can start to step back and ask ourselves why? This could either through pain caused by someone, or through jealousy of witnessing their successes. It is not their problem that we are triggered - we have to take radical responsibility for how we are feeling.

These soul contracts also bring a calmness, knowing the people you are meant to meet in your life have already signed a contract. We as humans, have free will, and every decision you make has the ability to shift your timeline of when you might meet the souls you are meant to meet, but you can't miss them. It's already written.

Spiritual Tools

As a child, one of my favourite movies was "Matilda", the one with
the little girl with magical abilities – if you haven't seen it, go, watch
it immediately! I also loved, "Sabrina the Teenage Witch", and
secretly hoped Melissa Joan Hart would be my older sister. The point
being, magic is all around us, and has been for centuries. I don't
necessarily believe you can point your finger and move things across
the room (not in this realm or lifetime anyways), but never say never!
I do, however, believe we all have the ability to access our magical
capabilities. I think like anything, learning a new skill takes practice,
and with practice comes confidence and a natural trusting in one's
abilities.

From the very basics of life and survival – you are magic. You
ingest food every day, you turn it into nourishment for your body, and
you transform it into waste and expel what doesn't serve your body
anymore. Literal, everyday magic! If your body has the power to do
that, just imagine what else you can do when you try to tap into your
magic.

The first time we do anything, we often stumble or fail. That
proves to our ego that we "can't" do it. A lot of people stop there,
and that's what the ego believes to be true, until proven otherwise.
When we create a practice of something, over time we get better and
better, and our ego starts to think, "oh, maybe we can do this". With
that comes confidence and the ability to trust in yourself, in your

abilities and your gifts. Sometimes this requires confirmation from a coach or energy practitioner to help teach you, reminding you how to access your magic. Sometimes it doesn't. Some people are born with the knowingness that they have magic or psychic abilities within them – there is no wrong way to tap into your magic. If you weren't born knowing, or weren't raised with examples around you of the possibilities, there are tools you can use to start to explore your magic.

Through this section I will share some of my favourites that I got started with. This is a brief summary of some of the many tools available to you. I am not an expert in any of these, but the world of spiritual tools can be quite overwhelming when you are looking for somewhere to start. I have included a list of other resources and experts on my website, *www.themavenproject.ca/bamresources* of the people and mentors that I admire, and have learned from. Feel free to follow any of them, and if they are listed on that page, I highly recommend their courses and offerings. There are also hundreds of other spiritual practitioners out there who, I'm sure, are equally incredible, that I have yet to experience their magic first hand. Trust yourself if you are drawn to someone's work! There's a reason their energy caught your attention.

Remember each person is different, so trust yourself when you are drawn to a certain section that there is something there for you. If you don't resonate with a section, that's okay, it's probably just not for you at this present moment. Each of these tools have come in phases for me, some I use consistently, others sporadically. You can come back to this section whenever you feel called. Sometimes, I find just flipping through a book to a random page will help me find the inspiration or confirmation that I need.

Meditation, Movement & Breathwork

Meditation can be as simple as going for a walk in nature with no distractions – leave your phone at home and just enjoy the walk. Allowing yourself to absorb the sights and the sounds, and let your mind wander. This is a great way to start to meditate, to start to see where your thoughts go, and to learn to bring yourself back to centre when you get distracted.

Meditation can also look like using a guided audio, or by sitting in silence for a few minutes. Meditation can look however feels best to you. It doesn't require fancy cushions, or headphones, but it can if that feels best for you. I have included a link to a guided audio meditation to help you tap into your energy on the resource page on the website. Meditation can also come through the use of music, listening to sound vibrations (such as sound baths), and through guided chanting using sounds like, 'om'. Those sounds will vibrate through your bodies, allowing your energy to recalibrate to different levels. Notice, if certain music or noise makes you feel on edge, and recognize that your body is telling you this is not a good energy for you at that moment. Also, notice what feels good, or what you crave more of. This is a great way to increase your vibrational energy – through the use of sound. You can find sound meditations online at the different hertz based on how you want to feel. Motivational or inspiring podcasts are also a great tool to tap into.

Movement through such activities like yoga or dance are great ways to start to move energy through your body as well. Simple activities to start to remind yourself of your mind and body connection, and ultimately your body and spirit connection.

Breathwork is a powerful tool you can use to connect to your body by taking a class or signing up for a course. There is so much power in our breath. You would think as humans, we innately know how to breath properly, but there's so much more power in our breath that we have barely tapped into. It's a great way to calm your nervous system, to come back to centre, and to clear your head. You can start simply by taking a deep breath in, and feeling the lightness enter your body. As you exhale, feel any stuck energy or heaviness move through you. Noticing where your breath gets stuck or pauses and just spending some extra time there.

Inhale love, and exhale doubt. Inhale peace, and release any anxiety that's stuck within your body. Slow, steady breaths. In through the nose, out through the mouth.

> **An Extra Dose of Magic**
> The Book, **Breath** by James Nestor, is a great read, explaining how our breath has changed over the years as we have evolved. Also, if you are called to do breathwork, be sure to find a trained facilitator. There is a lot of power in doing breathwork properly that can have transformational results.

Astrology & Astrocartography

Astrology is one of the most popular tools, as I'm sure you've seen or read your horoscope over the years. (If not, you can look up your sign based on your birthdate.) Typically, we are aware of our Sun Sign which is one of the 12 Zodiacs signs represented. For example, I am an Aquarius because I was born on January 30th.

> **Zodiac Seasons:**
> **Aries:** March 21 – April 19
> **Taurus:** April 20 – May 20
> **Gemini:** May 21 – June 20
> **Cancer:** June 21 – July 22
> **Leo:** July 23 – August 22
> **Virgo:** August 23 – September 22
> **Libra:** September 23 – October 22
> **Scorpio:** October 23 – November 21
> **Sagittarius:** November 22 – December 21
> **Capricorn:** December 22 – January 20
> **Aquarius:** January 21 – February 18
> **Pisces:** February 19 – March 20

There are three main signs you want to look for if you are wanting to start to understand your astrology. Your **Sun Sign** represents how you show up in the world. Your **Moon Sign** is how you show your emotions in the world, and your **Rising or Ascending Sign** is who you are here to be in the world. Each can offer different insights into why you are the way you are. Like all of these tools, this is simply a tool. If something doesn't resonate – leave it.

One thing I have found in doing this work is that before the age of 30, we often resonate more with our Sun Sign – as far as horoscopes or descriptions. After 30, we start to step more into our Rising Sign. So, if you are over 30, start checking out your Rising sign horoscopes and see if that resonates more! This also could be in conjunction with what is called our Saturn Return – which is where Saturn returns to where it was when you were born. Generally, this occurs roughly between the ages of 28-32. If you are not living your life on your terms or in alignment with who you truly are here to be this could be a very interesting time for you. Often things will shift drastically during this time period to push you to find a more authentic path. For me, this was the start of The Maven Project. Prior to this was when I was doing Interior Design, and I didn't realize until years later just how accurate the timing of it was to my Saturn Return.

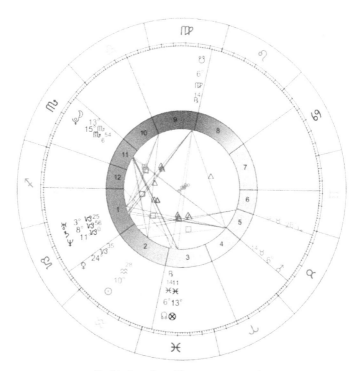

Ruth's Astrology Chart as an example.

Using your birthdate, birthtime and birth location you can find your Astrology Chart which goes into a lot more detail about where the planets were in the sky when you were born. This can offer insight into such things as your habits and behaviours, your passions and career opportunities for you. Using a tool like Astrology has given meaning and significance to why I do some of the things I do, why I am passionate or curious about different areas of interest and can act as a tool to help predict when to do certain things based on what is happening in your astrology chart. You can use Astrology from planning business launches by marketing to the themes we collectively go through, or to understand your children and how they are here to show up in the world. You can dive deeper into this, to understand world events, or how the planets affect the collective energies. To fully understand either of these charts, you can book an Astrology Reading with an Astrologist. I highly recommend booking a session to really start to understand what your Astrology is showing you. This is a tool that put into words things about me that I didn't know how to express otherwise.

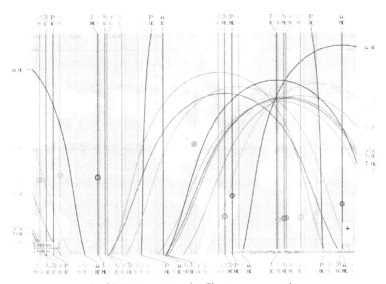

Ruth's Astrocartography Chart as an example.

You can also use what is called Astrocartography, to determine where in the world there are different points of significance for you. At a very basic level, it takes your astrology chart and overlaps it with a world map to see where the planets were when you were born. Wherever there is a line or an intersection of lines could be a place of significance to you. If you are looking to travel or move, this is a great tool. For instance, I knew I was being called to my Neptune line when I was trying to determine next steps in 2021. I knew I needed to be in a different location, and knew that this book was calling me to be written. Simultaneously, when I tapped in with friends to where I should go, I was being called to Florence, Italy. Of course, when I looked up my Astrocartography out of curiosity, my Neptune Line went directly through Florence. The Neptune Line offers qualities that inspire creative process and promote intuition – the majority of this book poured out of me while I was there.

As further confirmation, I am a third generation Florence (Florence Ruth Montgomery), named after my grandmother. I had rented an adorable place about 30 minutes outside of the city for two weeks with the intention of writing. The lady I stayed with had recommended a Reiki practitioner in the city of Florence, and when I called to book an appointment, she had Thursday, November 25th available. I thought, sure, I'll head into the city to spend the day and see it for the first time, and still have a few days back at the rental place before I moved to Florence to spend 3 days there exploring further. I had an incredible day in the city wandering, finished off by an amazing Reiki session. I woke up the next morning to a message from my mum, asking me if I knew that the day before was Grandma Florence's Birthday. I have never met her in this lifetime, she had passed before I was born, and November 25, 2021 would have been her 110th birthday – on the first day I was in Florence. I knew in that moment, that I was exactly where I was supposed to be.

Astrocartography can also be used to heal trauma or karmic ties from past lives, to offer insight into who you were previously, as well as to find places destined for you to learn a lesson in love, to experience peace, or to resolve conflict.

Moon Cycles

The moon offers a lot of wisdom and is a powerful tool in connection. There are two main ceremonies we can start to do to honour her essence and her energies around the New Moon and Full Moon.

New Moons are all about setting new intentions for the next cycle. This is a great time to practice your manifesting abilities. Write down what you would love to accomplish or call in over the next month. I love to do a good, better, best type of list. The Good is the things I will do, the tasks or projects or activities that are absolutely possible to do! The Better portion of the list is the things that would be ideal! Maybe that class I've been dreaming of taking, or that adventure I really want to go on, but just not quite sure of the logistics. And the Best portion of the list is the big dreams, like manifesting a goal income, making a new friend, or trying the thing that terrifies me. You get the idea, putting it out there that these are the things you'd like to call into your life. Whether it be new experiences, people, or an overall feeling of how you want to feel throughout the next season. There is no wrong way to do this. This act is about setting the intention for all of the good that is going to enter into your life over this cycle of the moon.

Full Moons are all about releasing what is no longer serving you. Where do you feel stuck? What do you want to finish up? This can be physical task items, energetic connections or feelings that are no longer serving you. Perhaps behaviours you keep repeating, or moments that you keep replaying in your head over and over. For Full Moons, you can do a Full Moon Ceremony around a campfire. Write down each item on an individual piece of paper that no longer serves you. If it is something or someone bigger, you can write a letter directly to that situation or person (with no intention of it ever being read by them) and get all of your feelings out.

Over a campfire, taking one piece of paper at a time, hold it to your heart, and I say:

"I release what no longer serves me.
I release (insert brief summary of what you wrote on the paper).
Thank you for the lessons and with so much love, I release you."

Then throw the paper into the fire and watch it burn. Fully watch it burn, letting it disintegrate and disappear. If you don't want to have a campfire, you can rip the paper into tiny pieces and flush it down the toilet as well. However, there is something very soothing about watching it go up in flames!

An Extra Dose of Magic
The moon cycles in 28-day periods. Women's menstrual cycles are also, on average, 28 days. Coincidence? I think not. There's magic all around us, most we don't even recognize but it's right in front of us. We are cyclical beings.

Dreams

Do you remember your dreams? We all dream, but we don't all remember our dreams. Your dreams can help your subconscious mind work through scenarios that you are experiencing or have experienced consciously. Especially in the 3-5 days leading up to a Full Moon, you may find your dreams are starting to get wild, or busy. It is your body's way of processing what no longer serves you, or it is offering clues into what may solve the problem.

You can start to play with your dreams. There are lots of interpretations of dream signs and symbols that you can look up. You can also start to set intentions before you go to bed, using your sleep as a helpful tool. For instance, if there's a problem you are struggling to solve, ask yourself to find a solution in your sleep just before you close your eyes for the night. Keep a journal beside your bed, and in the morning write down anything that came to mind or that you remember. It may not make sense at first, but you can look up the symbolism of what things mean. Our brain will use images of things we recognize to try to imitate a feeling or an understanding. With anything, if it resonates that's amazing, and if it doesn't feel accurate, trust that it's not. Start to play with it, and see what you can uncover and what connections you can make.

Witching Hour

Witching hour is that time between 3am and 4am. It is said that the veil between humans and the spiritual world is the thinnest. If you are constantly being woken up during this hour, your soul, your Spirit Guides or angels may be trying to talk to you. If this happens, keep a journal beside your bed and when you wake up next start journaling, asking "What do you want to tell me?" "What do you need me to know?" It feels odd at first as your ego or practical mind is trying to rationalize what you are doing, and like anything can take practice. Keep doing it, and eventually, you will start to understand the messages.

In the spirit realm they are so excited to talk to us, and forget that we are in fact here to be humans, and need sleep. Once you start to build a connection with them, you can start to remind them that you need sleep and please come back during the day.

Archangels, Guardian Angels & Spirit Guides

The other way that your Angels or Spirit Guides may start talking to you is through a ringing in your ear, through an itchy nose, or itchy palm. For me, randomly one of my ears will go silent, and the other will start to ring. This is my indication that someone is trying to communicate with me. When this happens, I grab a journal and start writing.

But what are they? Who are they?

The **Archangels** are energy beings that are accessible to us all. As mentioned before Archangel Michael is the Archangel of Protection. He is one of many that we can call on at any time for support, and they are available to us all, all the time.

121

Guardian Angels are your friends and family members that have passed. They are with you constantly if you need, looking out for you. They will often offer signs to let us know they are there in the form of dimes, feathers or animals. They can also show up in our dreams to let us know they are okay, or in a song on the radio just when you need it.

Spirit Guides are unique to each of us. You have your very own team of Spirit Guides. They are here when you need guidance or support, they will offer wisdom, or show you signs to point you in the right direction. You can connect with them by doing a Spirit Guide Meet & Greet or Introduction, often facilitated by another intuitive. Once that initial introduction has been made, you can connect with them any time. Much the same as meeting new people here in the human realm, the introduction to someone new, opens the conversation and connection, so you can build a relationship with them. Imagine going to a party solo and trying to meet people – it's more nerve-wracking and takes a huge amount of self-assuredness. Now, imagine going to a party with a friend who knows everyone there. They can take the pressure off by introducing you to people they think you would like.

Trust that everything happens for a reason. As humans we have free will, and our guides and angels will not interfere unless we ask for their support. Therefore, if you want support or guidance, you have to ask for it. Ask them to join you, ask them to show you a sign to know you are going in the right direction. And then trust what you see.

Have you ever been running late, maybe you misplaced your keys or knocked over your coffee on the way out the door? Just to get on the highway and pass an accident, knowing that if you had of been on time it could have been you? I believe that is someone on the other side protecting us, keeping us out of harm's way. Maybe they moved your keys, or knocked over your coffee. They won't offer support or guidance unless we ask, but they will protect us if we still have work to do as a human.

Last summer, I wrote, "I feel very disconnected from source, my guides. Yet when I asked, they simply said you are integrating and listening so intently, we don't need to come through with other messages. You are in it. Constantly." Know that even when it doesn't always feel like it, you are supported in all that you do.

Numerology & Signs From The Universe

Numerology is another great tool to get to know yourself on a deeper level. By using your birthdate, you can find out your soul number and your purpose for being here. You can also determine what karmic debt you need to master or repay in this lifetime, what your gifts are, what your destiny is and the path you are going to take to get there. It offers an amazing insight into who you are, and why you chose to enter this world on the date that you did. You can also use numerology by searching online the spiritual meaning of certain number sequences as you see them. Always remembering to take what resonates and leave the rest.

Numerology is also used to show up as signs from the Universe. The most common is when numbers will show up in repeating sequences, like 11:11 on the clock, or 555 in a license plate or phone number. These are often referred to as Angel Numbers. Each means something different, and is just a simple nod from the Universe to say, "I see you, you are not alone".

Again, this is a tool where you can work with a maven to read your personal Numerology. There are also some fantastic courses out there teaching Numerology and the depths of what you can use it for.

111 You are not alone.
You are fully supported & on the right path.

222 Trust the path that you are on.

333 You are being guided & supported right now.

444 You are divinely guided.
Look for signs from your guides.

555 Positive changes & shifts are coming!

666 A need to refocus your energy
Reconnect to yourself or your guides.

777 Lucky you!
Luck is on your side.

888 Abundance is coming!
You are aligned with the money you desire.

999 A cycle is coming to the end.
The closure you need to find the next step.

000 New beginnings.
A fresh start.

SIGNS FROM THE UNIVERSE
ANGEL NUMBERS

Oracle Cards & Tarot Cards

Oracle Cards and Tarot Cards are an excellent way to gain clarity around certain experiences or situations. You can pull a card, or do a card spread which offers insight into what you're struggling with or questioning. It can be as simple as, "What do I need to know today?" or "What is (this experience) trying to teach me?"

Oracle Cards are a great place to start, because you can pull one card all on its own and receive a message. Tarot Cards tend to take more practice because in traditional Tarot, depending how they lay, they each mean different things, and it can feel like a language all of its own.

In collaboration with four artists and two other co-writers, my company, The Maven Project, created an Oracle Deck perfect for beginners. It is called the "Daily Dose of Maven Magic Oracle Deck". Our intention with this deck was that some days a simple nudge is all you need, and other days, a shift in perspective, a powerful reminder of your magic or a divine message is necessary. These cards can be interpreted simply with their uplifting messages, yet they also have the power to connect directly to your soul with the message you didn't know you needed. The beauty of Oracle Cards is there is no wrong way to do it. Just trust that you are called to the right card for you.

It is the same with choosing a deck, trust that you will be called to find the deck that resonates with you. When you go into a shop that sells oracle or tarot cards, let your eyes wander, and see what you feel compelled to pick up. Often that is the deck for you at the moment.

When I first started playing with cards, I felt I had to always ask a friend who was more experienced with reading cards to pull one for me. Truth is, anyone can do this. The right card will find you. I encourage you to simply try! Like anything, the more you practice, the more confident you will become.

ONE CARD PULL

You can shuffle the deck,
choosing the top card or
whichever card falls out.

Or cut the deck in half,
choosing a card in the middle.

Or fan out the deck & choose
the card that calls to you.

YOU CAN ASK:

What do I need to know today?
What do I need to know about
(insert situation or person)?

THREE CARD PULL

Choose 3 cards from the top of the deck,
or at random or from breaking the deck
into three piles & choosing the
top card from each pile.

YOU CAN ASK:

What do I need to know today?
In the next 3 days?
In the next 3 weeks?

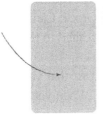  

CARD LAYOUTS + PROMPTS

Crystals & Pendulums

Crystals are a very personal thing as well, and when you need a crystal, you'll be drawn to the right one. I would recommend going into a crystal shop if you can and just see which ones catch your eye – which ones you are drawn to and trust that they are usually accurate.

Crystals are powerful healing tools, and can be used for all kinds of things. A couple of basic examples to get you started are to use quartz for clearing, rose quartz to open the heart chakra and amethyst to enhance your connection to source. Each stone generally represents the colour of the chakra they resemble. So, if you need throat chakra support you might be drawn towards blue crystals. If you need root chakra support you might be drawn towards red crystals, and so on.

There are some practitioners and healers that will use crystals in their practices as well. If you are feeling called to work with crystals, but don't know where to start, start there. Book a session with someone who uses crystal grids or crystal healing. And if you're asking, okay but where do I find someone? Start by deciding that you are looking for someone and ask the Universe to guide you. You will be amazed at who you are introduced to or what advertisements you see pop up in the coming days when you intentionally decide to try something.

You will also hear people talking about charging their crystals. If you have your own, it is a great practice to cleanse your crystals each month, by placing them under the full moon, to get an energetic cleaning. Note that some crystals are not meant to get wet, so instead of placing mine outside, I will often line my window sill with them. Trust what feels good to you.

Crystal Pendulums are a great tool to start to build your trust in your intuition. Again, trust what one you are called to. By holding it in your hand above your palm, you can hold it still, and ask a simple yes or no question to determine which way is yes or no for you. I always start by saying, "Show me Yes", thank you, "Show me No", thank you. Followed by an obvious yes or no question. If you are wearing a black t-shirt, ask "Am I wearing a black t-shirt?" and without moving your hands, the pendulum will either start to move back and forth or in a circle. Whichever way it moves, is how it will move when it's a yes for you. Then ask it a no question, like "Am I wearing a red t-shirt?" and it should move in a different direction. Once you determine which way is which for you, you can start to ask it some more difficult questions. For myself, a Yes is back and forth, and No is a clockwise circle, and a Maybe is a counterclockwise circle.

From experience though, the Universe will get annoyed. One time, when I was first playing with it, I was asking, "Will I meet the love of my life this week?" "Next week?" "Next month?" etc. Eventually the pendulum just stopped dead center and wouldn't move. It was like, you're being ridiculous and we're not doing this anymore.

You can also use your body as a pendulum. By standing with your feet shoulder width apart, place your hands on your heart and close your eyes. Take a deep breath in and ask a yes or no question. You will either naturally lean forward or backwards. Pay attention to which way is yes, and which way is no, and then start to ask your other questions. These are great tools to build trust with your intuition and confidence in your connection to source or Universal energy. The more and more we open up these channels of communication, the less tools outside of ourselves we need.

Connecting With Source & Your Psychic Abilities

As mentioned before, this can show up with a ringing in the ear, or an itchy palm or nose. This can also show up in what is often called "downloads". These are nuggets of wisdom from the five-dimensional world, sometimes from Universe or Source, your Spirit Guides, your Higher Self, or even your Inner Child. It may be a random thought that doesn't feel like yours. It may be a download for an offering you are meant to lead, or a course you are meant to take. It also happens, when you ask a question and get an answer that feels outside of yourself. The answers feel very truthful, without needing to understand the why or the how, it feels as obvious as if it were a fact you already know.

There are four main ways we start to develop our psychic abilities, called Clair Senses. None of these are better or worse than the other, but just like some people are visual learners and some prefer audio, each person has one that comes through the strongest. They may change over time as well, and you may have access to more than one!

- **Clairvoyance** means clear seeing. It is the ability to visualize, and to see into the past or future.
- **Clairaudience** means clear hearing. It is the ability to hear intuition, or downloads from outside of yourself.
- **Clairsentience** means clear feeling. It is the ability to feel energy, through goosebumps or chills or feeling like someone is there with you, feeling a presence.
- **Claircognizance** means clear knowing. It is the ability to feel intuitively, to get an intuitive hit do things a certain way without knowing why or how you know that.

I believe we all have the ability to tap into our intuitive gifts, like anything that requires skill, it takes time and practice, so be patient with yourself!

Sitting in silence or meditation is one of the best ways to start to tap into your gifts. Naturally one of the Clair Senses will be strongest for each of us, and I do believe, with practice we can access multiple ones. If there is one in particular that you would like to try, sit in silence (often in nature helps) and set your intention. For instance, "I would like to enhance my clairaudience abilities, please tell me what I need to know." And then listen. See what you hear or what thoughts come to mind, and trust that Source energy is with you. You could also further expand your intention by stating, "I welcome in any Spirit Guides, Angels, Archangels or my Higher Self to help me hear more clearly. I would like to enhance my clairaudience abilities, please tell me what I need to know." Listen, and trust that what you're hearing is meant for you.

You can also use any of the tools we touched on in this section to help you connect to yourself, and your intuitive gifts. The more self-aware you become, the more you will naturally start to trust your intuition, giving it permission to show up in new ways – such as visualizations, or hearing downloads. It takes time, but it will come!

Higher Self, Akashic Records & Timelines

Your **Higher Self** is the version of you that knows past, present and future. You can call on your higher support to offer guidance for next steps, to enhance your connection to Source. You can meet them through meditation, with a guide, or through energy work. With any of this work, by having someone hold space and support you, you are allowing them to make the introduction to show you what's possible.

"Your Higher Self is a piece of an all loving, all-embracing creative source. All you need to do is accept that this is not something external to you. It resides within you."

Wayne Dyer, Wishes Fulfilled

Think of it like meeting a new friend, it's tough to walk up to a stranger and introduce yourself, but if a mutual friend introduced you there is an immediate relaxation and ease. Just as you would use a Medium to connect with relatives or loved ones that have passed, your Reiki Practitioner, or Energy Healer acts as that mutual friend to call in your Higher Self, your Inner Child, your Spirit Guides and Archangels. Once the introduction is made it's easier to nurture that friendship all on your own. You can do it by yourself, but having an introduction allows you to skip some of the awkward small talk.

The **Akashic Records** is like a library to our past, present and future lifetimes. It is a history of our soul, like a library filled with all of our stories, from all of our timelines. The safest way to walk through these, are with a guide. Someone who can hold space to help you open your Akashic Records and help you to navigate through what you are seeing and experiencing. I have used these to gain glimpses into future moments in this lifetime, as well as past lifetimes to explore soul connections and contracts. There are so many options within this realm, it can be quite the journey, so having a guide is encouraged.

Sometimes when we do this work, we fast track a lesson. A lesson that we are meant to learn, may take years going about our day to day as a human. When we tap into Spiritual work, it can expedite the process.

It can feel like we've jumped timelines, or shifted paradigms. As a human with freewill, there are many options for how our lives will play out, depending on what decisions we make. When you are working with psychic energy and predicting or seeing any kind of future images it's important to remember that what you are seeing is based on the decisions you would make in that moment. If you went to a psychic and thought you were going to exit the building and go to your right during the appointment, you will see your future if you take that step. If you end up exiting the building and turning left, you have potentially shifted everything. I find it's important to see any of this future work as a possibility and not get too attached to the outcome. The other thing is if we get too attached, we stop living our lives as we normally would. For instance, if it was predicted that I would meet the love of my life in August, perhaps I would stop dating until then thinking, what's the point if I'm not meeting him until August? During the months leading up to meeting him, though, perhaps I was supposed to meet someone else that would have introduced me to him, and because I sat back and waited, I've shifted the timeline.

I believe we come into this life with a few main lessons, and one major timeline that we are meant to live out to learn those lessons. For some of us, that main lesson may take us 80 years to learn. For others, such as when we start doing personal development work, we can learn those lessons faster. When we do the deep healing work, we can jump ahead, collapsing time into a new reality. So, what could have taken 80 years to learn, may take 10 years for example. This then allows another timeline to play out, and essentially, we start stacking timelines together. Doing personal or spiritual development work, and becoming more self-aware, allows us to move through our blocks (or lessons) quicker. We are able to see that there actually is a lesson to learn. We can then acknowledge where we can adjust what we need to – whether that is in mindset, in actions, or simply in becoming aware of the lesson. Have you ever had a habit that you've never thought anything of and then one day someone acknowledges it, and all of a sudden you become aware of it, so you stop doing it? This happens with our lessons. Before becoming self-aware we hardly even notice the things we are doing. Once we can start to step back to see ourselves more fully, we can recognize that our habits or actions are actually the common denominator – therein lies the lesson for us.

For instance, have you ever had a friend that is dating someone that isn't good for them, and they finally break up, and you're like thank goodness! Only for them to start dating someone almost exactly the same after? When this happens it's because there is still a lesson in that situation for them and they aren't seeing it yet. It's like the Universe is saying, "Okay, let's try this again." Over and over until your friend, personally sees that that type of person isn't good for them – that's when the lesson is learned. When they are able to move onto a different type of partner, they have potentially completed the lesson in that timeline. We will always have lessons to learn, and timelines that can be worked through.

Paradigm Shifts happen when something pivotal happens to us. Perhaps it is someone sharing a perspective with you that completely changes the way you think or understand the world around you. Perhaps it is when you are given two options, and come to a fork in the road. If you choose option A, your life will look completely different than if you chose option B. This pivot point, creates a new reality – whether it be in who we are in relationship with, with our career, where we live, or in the opportunities available to us.

Returning from a deep healing session last summer, I was driving back to our family cottage, and although I've driven that road hundreds of times, it was like I was seeing it for the first time. It was the strangest thing, yet I immediately knew I was seeing things through a new level of awareness. It's like I had jumped timelines, and was integrating the new level within the drive, when my reality caught up to my new level of awareness.

Déjà vu also plays into this, there are many opinions of how this works, but currently, I believe there are two possibilities. The first is that when we experience déjà vu it's a little nod from the Universe that you are on the right track – you were meant to experience this, and it's like hitting a checkpoint in a videogame. The second is that, time is an illusion, and we are constantly operating on multiple timelines, and you've already been there before. It's, again, a checkpoint, to say yep, we've been here, with a glimpse into a different time when this same conversation or lesson, with the same soul happened.

With all of this the idea of time is fluid. Paradigms and timelines can intertwine with each other and overlap. Some lessons, we may learn in one timeline, and years later may show up again in a different timeline. This is when that lesson is potent for you to remember in order to become your next evolution of yourself. And often, we've been working through the same lessons throughout many lifetimes, so it will continue to come up to be healed or explored.

Past Lives & Generational Healing

For most of us, this is not our first-time experiencing life as a human – we have been here before. The belief in the spiritual world is that we come to Earth to learn. One of the past life healing sessions that I have had, believed that I originated in Atlantis and that I have experienced over 2000 lives since then. This is where the idea of an 'Old Soul' comes from.

Our past lives often influence our present lives, either by the lessons we need to learn and master in this lifetime, or patterns that we have engrained so deeply to protect us from events that happened in past lives.

For instance, I have struggled with a fear of being seen in this lifetime, due to multiple lifetimes as a witch where I was literally persecuted for showing my true self. This is the "witch wound" I referred to earlier. The fear runs so deeply that I have self-sabotaged my own success to avoid the spotlight, not intentionally, but reflecting back on it, it's obvious.

Past lives can vary so much and each experience will be unique. I have witnessed myself as a witch who was burned at the stake. In observing being taken to the burning, I had an overwhelming feeling of calmness wash over me. I knew in that moment that I was being burned because of the villagers' fear, not because I had done anything wrong. I had accepted my fate, knowing I had stood in my integrity in that lifetime.

In another past life, I witnessed myself running around a kitchen table in my nightgown as a little girl in what would have been the servant's kitchen. That version of me was loud and playful. She was giggling and having such a fun time. The past life then jumped ahead to myself as a young woman, in a ballgown, standing next to the fireplace in a very elaborate palace library. The interesting thing here, was I couldn't speak – it was like I was mute. This showed me that in order to keep my status of royalty, I was not to be boisterous, but to do as I was told and be a respectable, silent, woman. It was a sacrifice I made in that lifetime, that has come up in lessons in this lifetime to be seen and not heard.

In another past life, I was a scullery maid and I chose not to board the ship for that voyage. I had been having a romantic affair with the captain (which was not allowed). It turned out I was pregnant with his son, and intuitively I knew not to board that ship. The ship never returned and the captain died at sea. I was left to raise my little boy on my own, happily how I wanted to without my tarnishing my reputation.

Another time, I lost my two children in a house fire and I blamed myself. I have an irrational fear in this lifetime of leaving my hair straightener on, and will drive out of town only to return to double check that it is unplugged – it always is. This past life helped me to see why this fear is so large. I lost the things I loved most in a house fire in a previous life, of course I'm scared it may happen again.

Those are all just examples of what I have seen for myself. In these sessions, sometimes it's as if I'm transported back there and I am seeing exactly what's happening. Other times I am feeling the energy of what I would have experienced then. Every time there is a lesson that can be connected to what I am currently experiencing in this lifetime.

We also bring with us a lineage. We were born from our mother's womb, and she was born from her mother's womb. We carry with us in this lifetime rememberings of their past life experiences. We can look to our past lives and to our generational lineage to uncover different blocks, or lessons that we are holding onto that no longer serve us in this lifetime.

When working with past lives from my time as a witch, I have to remind my lineage and the past versions of my soul, that it is safe to be seen fully in this lifetime. The first time I did a generational healing, my ancestors tried to turn the healer away saying it's not safe, don't do it. The Healer had to energetically tell them it's okay for me to be seen in this lifetime, and in fact it will be celebrated this time. After some reassurance, the frustration and protective energy from my ancestors turned to a joyful celebration.

There are mavens that offer Past Life Regressions to help guide you to witness, heal and integrate your past lives. There are mavens that focus on Generational Healing to heal the wounds that your body carries with you to protect yourself and many that offer Akashic Record Readings.

Trust the Process

Not all of these ideas or ideologies may resonate, and again, that is okay. Take what jumped out at you, or what gave your stomach a little flutter. Perhaps, nothing did right now. That's okay – take your time. Perhaps, you're lit up and excited about all of them! One step at a time remembering that you don't have to do all the things, right this second. This is a journey of self-discovery, let it unfold as it's meant to. If you are seeing resistance show up, perhaps now isn't the time. For instance, if you are trying to book a session with someone, and it just keeps getting rescheduled, trust that that Practitioner or that Modality isn't for you right now. There are a lot of beautiful practices out there that I did not mention as well. If you start to hear about the same modality from different sources, trust that the Universe is nudging you to explore it!

You don't need to do all the things, but you can do multiple things at once.

Stepping Into Purpose

Purpose. The ever-elusive purpose. What is your purpose? Why are you here? I think we all have multiple purposes, and they evolve over time as our passions change. I think our purpose is simply in being here to experience this life. Whatever you do with your purpose, is up to you. It's time to release the narrative, that you have to do, be or create something incredible in this lifetime.

> "The feeling of being lost and not knowing my
> purpose is like so many people. Being lost
> and the lessons you gain is your purpose.
>
> **Your story is your purpose.**
> **It's not one thing. It's everything.**"

Ruth Montgomery, November 2018 Journal Entry

What if your purpose, is simply to be here?
To be here now.
To be present to the life around you, without needing to know what's next.
Taking time each day to simply be;
Be with your thoughts.
Be creative.

Be open and see where your mind wanders.

To be here now, with yourself and for yourself; to become self-aware.

To be present, to be mindful, to be aware, to be awake, to be healthy.

To be present in the quiet hours of the morning. To be listening in the depths of your dreams.

To be here now. That is your purpose.

To embrace each moment. The good for the memories. And the not so good for the lessons.

The simple joy of being alive. Take a breath. How does that feel?

The simplicity of taking in the sunset, of the sound of the water crashing against the shore.

The calm and the chaos.

The unkept and the beautiful.

Your purpose is a place to be. Simply as you are. No more. No less.

Just here in this moment.

What if that is your purpose?

Living your best life or living your life on purpose, doesn't have to be big. It doesn't have to be this world-changing, life-altering accomplishment. It just has to be *happy*.

Happy, by definition, is "feeling or showing pleasure or contentment". Being content is defined as being in a state of peaceful happiness. Therefore, to be content, is to be happy and to be happy, is to be content. Simple. Yet, we often over complicate that.

This feeling that our life has to be big, and exorbitant and changing lives, is out-dated. By you being in your purpose, as we defined above, you allow others to show up in theirs. You allow others to find happiness in contentment. In being.

That's the purpose. And if you happen to do, be or create more out of that place of purpose, that's amazing too. But it doesn't need to be the goal. It *gets* to be part of the ripple of your purpose.

So, how do we show up in purpose? How do we show up on purpose?

Journaling: Gratitude & Intentions

Seeing the beauty in where you are in this moment and finding gratitude for the things around you is one of the best ways to stay in your purpose. By showing up with gratitude, you welcome in more to be grateful for. That energy and vibration of your calm happiness will attract the right people and opportunities that will become the stepping stones within your purpose.

Journaling has been one of the best tools in my toolbelt for getting to know myself better. I regularly interchange the wording spiritual awakening with the journey to self-awareness. I often think they are one in the same. The more we awaken to ourselves, the more self-aware we become. And the more self-aware we become, the more authentic our purpose starts to feel.

An easy way to start journaling is to start with lists of gratitude, starting to see the world around you with a grateful heart. Not just for the big moments, and celebrations. But the simple things, like my hot cup of coffee this morning, or the gentleman that held the door for me today. If it feels overwhelming, at the end of the day, start with just one thing you are grateful for. And speak it out loud or write it down. Then when that becomes habit or easier at least, start to expand your list to three to five things each day. The more and more we do this, the more you will start to be able to see it with gratitude as it is happening. The more self-aware you will become.

Setting intentions, is another great way to start journaling, and to start living in your purpose. What are your intentions for the day? We often create to-do lists, and then get discouraged when we don't complete them. As you know we are human beings, not human doings. How can you be in the world today? Start by setting your intentions for how you want to be or feel. What is your intention for the day? For example, I will experience today through love. I use intentions to set my energy for the day, in a "I only have time for positive energy today" kind of way.

Throughout my travels in November 2021 in Europe, my mantra each day of travel was "It gets to be easy and effortless. I only have space to meet kind and loving humans that are showing up for my greatest and highest good." And it worked. I had some of the smoothest travel days, I was greeted by kindness and like-minded people everywhere I went.

I also use intentions, say before a tough meeting, or before a social gathering where I may normally get triggered or annoyed by people, saying "Today is going to be full of positivity and enjoyment. I am full of love. I exude love." And you know what? On those days – I don't get triggered, because I have set my intention for the day. It's like an internal guideline of where we are allowing our energy to be on the scale today. The same triggers may show up, but because I have set my intention to show up in the vibration of love, I react from the vibration of love.

Journaling, as you can see throughout this book, has offered insight into my mind that I wasn't even aware of until I took the space to write it down. You can start with a "Dear Diary" aspect and write about your day. Slowly starting to shift from the "doing" to the "being" energy. Allowing yourself time to reflect on how things made you feel. It takes time. To write this book I went back through my old journals over the last 7-8 years. Some took over a year to fill, others less than two months. Now that journaling has become a habit, I know that when I am avoiding journaling, it's because there is something happening in my daily life that I'm not ready to acknowledge or reflect on yet. With any of these tools as you start to build a level of self-awareness. You start to also be aware in the absence of it.

When I don't journal for a while, I know a shift is coming. For me, I know that I am avoiding it. Sometimes, because it will be uncomfortable, and other times because it will require me to sit with big emotions and process the emotions associated with whatever lesson it is. I have to remind myself still that we have the most growth in the uncomfortable. I promise you as you move through this work, it doesn't necessarily get easier, but you will be able to move through the uncomfortable quicker. When it feels like you are in the midst of a lesson, use the mantra *gratitude on good days, and trust on bad days*. Trust that it will all work out exactly as it's supposed to – even when it's uncomfortable.

Journaling is a great tool to help release your energy and emotions. It helps you to physically move through it by putting it on paper, and getting it out of your mind. It's still there for you to refer back to at any time, but it doesn't need to take up space in your body anymore.

I suggest you try free flow writing. This allows your mind to get out of the way, and for all of your thoughts to be released. Free flow writing is writing with the intention of writing whatever comes to mind, without editing. When we type on a computer or phone, there tends to be a disconnect and we will re-write or edit as we go. When you write by hand, pen to paper, you can get into more of a flow state – but any writing is better than none, regardless of which method you use. For myself, writing in a free flow style with pen to paper, I think has been the biggest catalyst to my growth. Writing without reading as you go, allows your soul to express itself. When we re-read and edit as we go, we can get into our ego and judge what we're writing by thinking things like, "don't write that, that sounds stupid" or "that doesn't make any sense, what are you even talking about?" When you write without that pause or critique, you can start to get really clear on what your soul is trying to tell you. If this feels too difficult, or unnatural, journal prompts are another great way to start to explore what you're really feeling.

Journal Prompts for Self-Awareness:
1. What in your daily life excites you?
2. If money weren't a factor, how would you spend your days?
3. What are your strengths?
4. What are the traits you wish you could love more?
5. What do you admire in others that you wish you had?
6. What experiences do I need to forgive?
7. How am I holding myself back?
8. What do I love about myself?

---

9. What dream do I wish I could experience?
10. What is on my heart?
11. How do you want to feel?
12. How do you want to be remembered?
13. Are you currently living like you want to be remembered? What would you change?
14. What does happiness for other people, look like to you?
15. What does happiness for you, look like to you?

Once you are done writing, then you can go back and read. It can be really cool to see what comes up. For instance, one time I was writing in a free flow state and I was following some journal prompts. The question was, "what do you love to do?" and I wrote, "I love to run". This was a moment, where I had to put my pen down, re-read, and laughed out loud thinking "wtf? I do not love to run, where did this come from?" Somewhere, within me, I am a runner. That version of me is deep down there somewhere screaming to come out apparently, so someday, I know I will consider myself a runner. I know this to be true, and if you know me currently, you know this is not the truth at the moment. It was a great reminder of just how much our soul knows, and wants to communicate with us – even if I'm not ready to be a runner just yet.

An important part of the processing piece is to reflect back on what you have written, and the lessons you have learned. This can be done days, weeks or even years later. When you take the time to reflect back or re-read old journals, you can start to see themes, or lessons. When you are in certain situations, it's hard to see what the lesson is, but looking back we can see what was learned. I have started to make this part of my end of year ritual. I re-read my journal entries from the year, and make a list of any patterns, or things that stood out to me. It can be really cool to see just how far you've come over the year. Or to notice, where there is still something you keep journaling about – there may be more work to be done there.

Opportunities & Abundance

You don't have to live a mediocre life if you don't want to. I believe, life is too short for mediocre. Being content is okay and some people will never want more. You can want more for them, but you can't force it – that's their decision. You do however, get to decide what a mediocre or abundant life looks like to you.

Does this look like flying First Class, and jet-setting around the world with all of the time and financial freedom you could imagine? Or does an abundant life, simply mean enjoying coffee with a friend, and having the time to take a walk on the trails near your home? Like many things in this life, abundance can be as simple or as complicated as you make it. The reminder here is that life *gets* to be abundant.

Before we can call in more abundance, I believe we have to see the abundance we are currently surrounded by. A good exercise is to journal all of your accomplishments, and blessings, to see how truly abundant you already are. Stepping into that state of abundance, allows more abundance to enter. Romanticise your life. Find the magic that already exists.

Start by making a list of all of the things that feel or have felt abundant in your life. It could include things like; kissing, cuddling, the taste of the ocean, new food, and so on. Noticing what is on your list, how can you start to do more of what you've already experienced? Use this as an opportunity to start to magnify the greatness of your current life. That way you can start to expand your energy to accept new levels of abundance into your life.

If abundance feels off for you, or you can't imagine an abundant life, choose joy. What brings you joy? Start there, and the abundance will follow. Start to see the beauty in being in a state of joy. *"I see the beauty in everything."* Maybe joy shows up when you're having coffee with a friend, wine on a patio, a walk on the trails, or watching the sunset on the beach. Simplicity is key here – don't over complicate it; enjoy and embrace the simple things.

"I feel so much peace and inner joy. Not all areas in my life are full but the parts and the people in my life are."

Ruth Montgomery, September 2019 Journal Entry

What if you want more? Start to look beyond your needs, and what you truly desire in this life. Ask from your heart: what do you want? Take the chance on yourself. Money gets to flow to you easily and effortlessly if you choose. Often this comes down to worthiness, thinking we are worthy or not of a life of our dreams. Money is energy, and when our basic needs are met (like suggested in Maslow's Hierarchy of Needs), we can start to see that it is simply another form of energy. Money does not define our worth.

However, at first glance, the things we want often do cost money. Let's dig a little deeper, and look beyond the narrative society has taught us. There are so many ways to bring things into your life, without money:

- Who do you know that has connections to the thing you want? Ask them if they can connect you.
- Who do you know that has or has done the thing that you want? Ask them for tips or what they would suggest.
- What skills do you have that you could exchange for the thing or experience that you want?
- Where else have you seen the thing or the experience that you want? Try asking for it. A chair for instance, say you have a particular colour of chair in mind that you desire, ask your friends or social media following if they know anyone that has one that they are looking to get rid of. Perhaps someone has been holding onto that chair because it's in too great of condition to throw out, but they don't need it anymore and would love to see it go to a good home.
- Manifest it by asking for what you want. Put it out into the world, and ask to be shown the answers. The "how" will figure itself out.

"A daydream is a dream seed. A seed imagined
before it becomes a reality. Anything you
can imagine you can create."

Ruth Montgomery

If you can't find the opportunity you're looking for, create it! Book the dream trip, go to the events out of your comfort zone, engage in conversations and ask lots of questions. Start to surround yourself with people who want more than a mediocre life. And continually do it with gratitude. As Elizabeth Gilbert in *Big Magic* wrote, "You will never be able to create anything interesting out of your life if you don't believe that you're entitled to at least try."

Repeat after me: Thank you, Universe, for providing me with what I need and the opportunities that best suit my desired life. It gets to be easy and effortless.

"When you see an opportunity,
it is up to you to jump."

Alex Banayan, The Third Door

What have you always wanted to try? What opportunities would you love to create? Imagine those big bucket list items, the crazy ones that feel nearly impossible. Putting yourself out there and stating your big, audacious goals is one of the most vulnerable things you can do.

What if you fail? What if people mock you? What if it doesn't happen? You could go on for days.

But what if it works? What if you succeed? What if it happens faster than you can possibly imagine?

There is so much power in voicing what you want. Putting it out into the world, and letting the Universe take over. For example, something that had been on my bucket list since I was little and used to watch "I Love Lucy" on repeat, was to go grape stomping! I had connected with the owners of a winery and had purchased wine from them for previous events, simply because I loved their wine, and they were local to me. I presented the idea of partnering with them to offer grape stomping at a future event. They thought it was a great idea, but weren't able at the time to come to the event. Voicing that idea out loud to them, opened up the conversation and allowed them to offer to let me pick grapes from the vines to use for my event. The owner of the winery even met me on site the day before my event, and helped me collect enough grapes to fill two buckets worth for grape stomping for our couples' retreat. Had I not had the bravery to share my idea, it would still be on my bucket list today.

Manifesting: Affirmations & Visualizations

Manifesting is the idea of calling in what you desire. Imagining what you know to be true in your life right now, and dreaming of what you want to be true for you in your future.

> "Imagination is everything. It is the
> preview of life's coming attractions."
>
> Harriette Jackson

We can only imagine what we've seen somewhere else. If you can imagine it, you can create it for yourself. Perhaps you know someone else who is doing what you want to do, perhaps you've seen it in a movie, or even in a past or future life of your own. If you can imagine it, it can be for you.

This works for our mind in reverse as well. If you believe something to be true and keep telling yourself it, you will create that. For instance, if you are constantly saying I am broke, the Universe hears that and thinks, "ah they want to be broke! Broke it is!" Our words and thoughts are very powerful, we can absolutely create our own reality. The Universe hears you, and responds.

Manifesting has allowed me to see The Ellen DeGeneres Show live twice, to cruise with Oprah, and I was scheduled to attend the Queen of England's Garden Party before she passed – all because I put it out in the world, and took the steps to show The Universe that I was serious.

Let's start with Ellen. To get tickets to see her show as an audience member, you have to enter into a lottery of sorts. They list the dates up to three months in advance, opening a week of dates at a time. First of all, you have to pay attention to that, if you want specific dates. Then you must actually submit your request, and then you wait. I was attending Lori Harder's event, 'The Bliss Project' in March of 2018 and knew I would be in Los Angeles with a window on either side of the event to see the Ellen Show. I applied, and heard nothing for months. Assuming I had missed it, as it was my 6th time applying, I believe. I know people that have applied upwards of 40 times, and still never got tickets. It was a month or so later, coincidently on January 29th that I got an email saying, "Congratulations! You've got tickets!" Five of us went to the show, and that day happened to be an odd taping day. They were doing half of two shows, so it was an extended taping time. Due to the adjustment in the schedule, Ellen herself, came out and did a Q&A period with the audience at the end. A few people asked questions, before one brave woman, got up and asked if we could all come back for the 12 Days of Giveaways! Those are Ellen's event days leading up to Christmas, where the audience each goes home with thousands of dollars' worth of gifts or prizes. It was a big ask, and Ellen got really quiet. She took a moment and said, "if you're going to ask questions like that, we're going to have to stop the Q&A" (pause for dramatic effect) "because yes! You can all come back!" Mic drop. Ellen left the studio with the audience erupting in cheers, trusting the producers to figure out the logistics of getting all of our contact information. All because one woman asked for it. What a wild ride. The five of us all got tickets to return in November of 2018 for Day Two of Twelve Days of Giveaways! So, not only did we see Ellen once, but twice we manifested it.

In between shows, a friend had sent me an article sharing that Oprah was hosting a Girls' Getaway Cruise to the Bahamas on January 30, 2019 (My 30th Birthday). I think the cruise dates were announced in June, and I found out about it in August of 2018. Of course, the cruise was fully sold out by then. I called the cruise line and asked what my options were. I talked to a very nice woman, named Deborah and tried to find out how I could get on that cruise. I asked if she had any pull as an employee or if she knew anyone, I was trying whatever I could because you only live once, right? Deborah was lovely, and told me my best option was to sign up for the waitlist and pay a fully refundable deposit to hold my spot. She said chances were slim, but you never know.

Fast forward to January 2019, I still hadn't heard from the cruise line. I had called a couple of times to check in and see where I was on the list, and they couldn't tell me due to privacy policies. It was my champagne birthday (when you turn the age of your birthdate – I was 30 on the 30th) so I started making other plans. I had a Mastermind Retreat to attend in Destin, Florida the week before my birthday with my business and spiritual coach, so I started there. I realized I was only 3 states away from having been to 30 of the states in the U.S.A. and decided to make that my goal to celebrate instead of the Oprah cruise. 30 States by my 30th birthday. I also made plans to be home the day after my birthday to drive to Boston with girlfriends to have a weekend getaway. (Note: This is not my average birthday, but for a big milestone like that - I celebrate my birthdays the way I think they deserve to be celebrated.) Something in me, for whatever reason, could not seem to book the hotel for Boston and I left for Florida trusting it would work itself out.

Off I went, starting in Florida for the retreat, then renting a car to drive to Montgomery, Alabama to Jackson, Mississippi and finally, my 30th state, New Orleans, Louisiana where I visited friends for a couple of days. I started the almost 9-hour drive on January 29, 2019 back to Orlando, Florida where I had made plans to visit a friend and go to Disneyworld for my birthday. Keep in mind, I'm Canadian and was relying on wi-fi to have cell service. Wouldn't you know, I pulled into a rest-stop/welcome centre at 11:11am and just as I turned on my phone, a call came through. The man on the other end of the phone said, we have a room available for you on Oprah's Girls' Getaway Cruise, we depart tomorrow, are you still interested? Yes, yes, yes! Yes, I am! I called my mum quickly to see if she wanted to join me for the cruise. She was able to find a flight from Toronto, Canada to Fort Lauderdale, Florida for early the next morning in order to meet me. I still had to drop off my rental car in Orlando, so I snuck in a birthday breakfast with a friend before catching a quick flight to Fort Lauderdale to meet my mum in time to cruise! I got to spend my 30th birthday onboard a cruise ship with Oprah, and 2,500 of her closest friends (fans). When we checked in, and told them that we had just found out yesterday we had a room, they were shocked. They said the waitlist was over 1,200 people. The cruise was a 3-day cruise, meaning I missed my flight home, and was in the middle of the ocean, when I had intended to be driving to Boston. Of course, my girlfriends completely understood the change of plans and trusted that it all happened exactly as it was supposed to.

Seeing the magic of January 29th for me, I decided to try for a third time in 2020. As a Canadian citizen, a passport holder of a Commonwealth Country, at that time you were allowed to apply to go to the Queen of England's Garden Party at Buckingham Palace. You get one opportunity to go, and once you've been once, that's it. It is also a random draw, in a very hard to find online application. I had found the application and knew it opened at the end of January. A friend and I both applied on January 29th to double our chances. Wouldn't you know weeks later, she received the email saying we had an invitation waiting for us! Due to the dynamics of 2020, we were unable to go unfortunately. Perhaps we'll attend a different garden party in the future.

Manifesting doesn't have to be that bold all of the time, but it's fun to dream big and see what you can create. It can be much simpler. A cool trick I like to try when I'm playing with manifesting, and the power of my words is when I'm driving. Telling myself I will find a parking spot close to the store I am going to. Saying or thinking that over and over as you are approaching the store you are going to. You will be amazed at how often it happens. When it doesn't work, honestly think about it, did you actually ask for a parking spot close to the store you were going for? Or did you ask for a parking spot? Get super specific for specific results.

A great example of this is also when driving, if you are constantly saying or thinking, "I'm going to be late! Shit, I'm going to be late!" And you continue to hit every red light. The Universe doesn't hear positive or negative words, it simply hears "late" and thinks "oh, they want to be late, here I'll keep giving them red lights!" Next time you are running late, try saying something like; "I am on time", "I have lots of time" Or "I am only available for green lights today" - and see if you can manifest green lights this way instead!

When dreaming up your big, beautiful idea, be sure to state something along the lines of "This is what I want or better". This allows you to put your intention out there to say this is what I am envisioning, but removes the control. In this you are trusting that the Universe knows you best, and knows what is coming. If we limit ourselves to saying, this is what I want, and this is how I am going to get it, often we are disappointed because that *thing* wasn't really meant for us. Generally, in an abundant mindset, the outcome is better than we can imagine. By saying "I want this *or better*", it's kind of like saying, "okay your turn Universe, show me what you've got for me!" (For more on this see page 224 for *A Thought on Goal Setting*).

Another way to tap into purpose is to manifest by using affirmations and visualizations.

Affirmations are a positive tool that can be used to motivate you, to remind you of your worth, to influence your subconscious mind, and to help you achieve your goals. Some people choose to use affirmations daily to remind yourself of certain things, or to call certain events into your life.

Some of my favourite affirmations are:

- I am worthy of love.
- I am unlimited in my wealth - all areas of my life are abundant and fulfilling.
- I am calm & focused in all that I do.

Affirmations can sometimes feel far from the truth as we're starting to reprogram our subconscious beliefs. If you aren't currently wealthy, and you keep telling yourself, "I am wealthy" your conscious mind says, 'hey wait a minute that doesn't feel true'. Sometimes by saying the thing your conscious mind believes to be untrue over and over can cause confusion, and creates a lack of trust within your body. If what you're saying to yourself feels foreign or untrue, try using the words "I will be wealthy." It switches the statement from present truth to future truth. You can also switch it to, "May I be wealthy?" – this poses the question as an option to your mind. And it gives the mind time to digest the possibility.

It's also important not to put qualifying statements to your affirmations. You can say "I am happy" as present tense, instead of saying "I will be happy when...". This implies you still have work to do to be happy, and that you are not happy currently. Keep it simple, and just say, "I am happy" or "I will be happy." Full sentence. We regularly try to over explain and justify ourselves, but for the purpose of affirmations, we want it as simple as possible.

Try writing your affirmations on sticky notes, and placing them on mirrors or spots throughout your home. If it feels too silly, and you don't want people to see, try sticking them inside cupboards you use every day, or inside your medicine cabinet. Little hits of inspiration to start your day on a positive note.

Where affirmations help us to feel into our manifestations, visualizations help us to see what we want to bring into our lives.

"As every architect or designer knows, there is a critical step between vision and reality. Before imagination becomes three dimensional it usually needs to become two dimensional. It's as though the unseen order needs to come to life one dimension at a time."

Glennon Doyle, Untamed

This can be done in your mind by sitting in quiet reflection or meditation, and visualize what you want to see, have or experience in the future. If you want to speak on stages, imagine yourself on a stage. Picture the faces in the audience looking back at you, feel the energy of the full auditorium, and see the shining lights in front of you. Picture what you are wearing and visualize the microphone in your hand. If you see yourself having children someday, imagine yourself with your children, see how many you have, picture them smiling back at you, and imagine playing with them.

You can also create a vision board. This is a popular tool using images from magazines, or the internet. Print out or draw different words, emotions, or goals to accompany the various images that make up your ideal future. There are two ways you can do this. The first way is to create your vision board and put it up where you can see it every day. Putting it right in front of you, so that you can see it each day and become familiar with it. The second is to create it, and put it away. Out of sight, out of mind. And check back in in a few months, and be amazed at what you brought into your life.

The point of a vision board, not only helps you see it for yourself, but it also allows you to declare it. Saying "hey Universe, this is what I want! I trust you to support me in achieving all of these items". Knowing that you are putting it out into the world you can start to take inspired action to create your dream life.

This is not some magic spell where you put it out into the world and carry on doing things as you've always done and expect miraculous changes to occur. You actually have to do the work. You have to show the Universe that you are serious. You are willing to do some of the work, and trust that the Universe will figure out the rest of the "how". For instance, you want a cottage on the lake? Start talking to a realtor or mortgage broker to see what it is going to take to be able to purchase one, and to start to look at cottages. This is your first step in manifesting that cottage. You want to speak on stage? Call your dream location and see what it would cost to book that venue for a night. Figure out the logistics – how many people does it seat? Do you need to bring in your own lighting experts or does the venue provide that? Start to immerse yourself in that world and learn how it works. Call or message your favourite event planner or conference, and ask how you get on their stage. What does it take? What do they look for in a speaker? How can you attend one of their events, and introduce yourself to the organizers? You get the idea. Start to explore what it would take to make your visions a reality. The Universe will see this and respond, thinking, oh she's serious! And be sure to say yes when opportunity presents itself.

I had a moment last summer with Sophie, my pet pig – who has the attitude of a small toddler – where she would not stop talking. I was trying to get work done, and she just kept grunting, on and on. I had filled up her water dish, she had already had breakfast, she had been outside to pee, and for a walk. I could not figure out what she wanted or needed, and I felt helpless, and exhausted from her chatter. I remember yelling at her, "I can't help you if you don't know what you want!" And as the words came out of my mouth, I had to laugh. I had the feeling of the Universe saying, 'see how it feels? I can't give you what you want, if you don't tell me what you want'. Pets, and children can be such beautiful reminders and mirrors of what lessons we need to remind ourselves of. Pay attention to those moments too, because the Universe will try to connect to you through things you already know.

When you're starting to actively manifest, it's important to remember that some things may not happen on your timeline. There are sometimes other lessons you need to learn first, so keep your belief strong, and don't give up hope! When in doubt of your future, be grateful for your present.

Manifesting may also not appear in the way you imagined. As an example, imagine you are trying to call in money and abundance and the feeling of financial independence. Often, we imagine this as business success, or coming up with a great idea that is an overnight success. We see money pouring in. We can get such tunnel vision, that we miss the fact that money comes to us in a variety of ways. Perhaps, it shows up when someone pays for your coffee in the drive-through line. This could be present in the support of a partner who has a great paying job which allows you to follow your passions without stress. We want the money to be ours, but we are being offered financial freedom in a different way. With manifesting, get clear on what you want to bring in or what you want to feel, but leave the how to the Universe. Let the "how" show up in unexpected magical ways!

> "I don't know what I am here to do and I won't fully until
> I can look back and see all that I've accomplished. But I can
> manifest the lifestyle and the feelings I want to, now."

> Ruth Montgomery, February 2019 Journal Entry

Love & Finding Yourself

Finding your purpose is ultimately about getting to know yourself. About creating a level of self-awareness that invites in the highest vibration of love. When we are in our feminine energy, we give with ease. Receiving tends to be harder. We need to learn to give and receive equally, yet our focus often shifts towards giving to others and we neglect ourselves in the process.

An Extra Dose of Magic

Think about the last time someone complimented your outfit. Did you simply say 'thank you', and receive the compliment? Or did you automatically, say 'oh I got it from (insert store), I've had it for years?'

We are quick to deflect compliments and small gestures. The last time someone offered to grab the door for you, or to help carry something, did you allow them the opportunity to support you and say 'thank you'? Or did you stand in your independence, and say, 'it's okay, I've got it'?

When we say no to these small moments, we are actually robbing the other person from having the ability to give to us. It's so easy to give compliments, or to offer support to others, but when it comes to receiving, a lot of people tend to struggle.

Learning to love ourselves, truly love ourselves, requires knowing yourself. And how do you get to know someone you want to fall in love with? You date them!

Start by taking yourself out on a date. Like a real date, pull out all the stops, get dressed up, do your hair, whatever you would normally do – treat yourself like you were meeting the love of your life for the first time!

> "You can't love yourself fully,
> if you don't know yourself truly."
>
> Ruth Montgomery

If the thought of this feels overwhelming start with something small – like going for a walk by yourself, go get ice cream or watch the sunset. Taking yourself to a movie, all by yourself is also a great place to start. It seems so simple, yet the majority of people I've asked have never done it, and are shocked at the idea of it. It is liberating, I promise you. After the initial nerves of walking in solo and thinking everyone is watching you, it's easy. The lights dim and everyone is in their own little bubble. The darkness allows you to relax into yourself lessening the fear of others watching you. You have two hours to just be with yourself. By the time the lights come up, you realize no one else is judging you, or perhaps even considering why you're there alone. You feel inspired, and empowered. It's a simple act, but one that will leave you feeling so sure of yourself. You could also try taking an art class, taking yourself to the spa or go visit an aquarium or a museum. A place where you have something to focus on outside of yourself, to help ease the pressure of the date.

When you're ready – take yourself out for dinner at a nice sit-down restaurant, alone and with no distractions. It's easy when you can mindlessly pass the time by scrolling on your phone, but try to take the time to look around, to relax into being there, sitting with your own presence. Be mindful of your thoughts, and get curious with where your mind goes.

It's so crazy the thoughts that go through your head while sitting by yourself. I have taken myself on dates many times, and honestly, going to the movie theatre solo is one of my favourite things to do. Last summer, I enjoyed a glass of wine and wood-fired pizza on a patio at a winery solo. During this date, I purposely witnessed where my mind went. Our minds are fascinating. It so quickly flits from "I'm SO proud of myself for taking myself out on a date." To "What do I do with my hands?" "Are they looking at me?" "Should I play on my phone?" "Is there anything new on my phone?"

Simply "being" is a practice. It takes time. It takes repetition. It takes grace. Patience. Self-love. Self-compassion. Gosh what a beautiful privilege to be able to practice this. To be alone.

"I will miss these days. I will miss these moments.
I am here now. As lonely as single at this age can be.
I will miss this. I will make a point of continuing these "dates"
whether it can be a meal out, a night at a hotel,
or a movie by myself. I will continue to "date" myself
and "be" okay with myself.
As hard as it becomes, this is a priority."

Ruth Montgomery, A Letter to Myself, Summer 2021

When you are comfortable doing that, I highly encourage you try traveling alone. Maybe it's a night away at a hotel, or a trip across the world. You will feel extremely vulnerable when you have no one else to ask questions, or to rely on. But when you have the realization, that you in fact, are perfectly capable all on your own, you will be living high on life for days! If something doesn't go according to plan, you adapt. There is nothing to be fearful of, but start with baby steps. No one is judging you in these moments but yourself.

It's a very powerful lesson, to observe where your judgements come up. Why are you judging yourself for that? Would you judge someone else for that same thing? What part of you felt vulnerable and insecure? Did you feel unsafe? Did it trigger something in you?

It's important to celebrate the wins during these experiences as well. Where did you feel empowered? Did that surprise you? What did you do, that you wouldn't have thought you could do on your own?

Knowing our own strengths, and weaknesses help us to grow and accept ourselves for who we are. You are a beautiful soul and yes, I'm sure you're not perfect – me either. What we perceive as imperfections are often the things that set us apart. When we can own those qualities and shift them into an awareness, being vulnerable isn't so scary anymore. The things we are often fearful of others judging us for, become empowering, not dismantling.

The key with all of this is to try not to distract yourself during your solo date. It can be intimidating to be out in a world that is curated for couples, and it takes a courageous person to start to explore that. Be gentle with yourself, one baby step at a time.

Finding Yourself In Relation To Others

Connection is vital to our human existence. We need it to flourish. We need family and friends, or friends that feel like family. We need touch points with other humans to know we're not alone.

We also need intimate relationships. Places where we can be vulnerable and where we can be completely ourselves. With people who are willing to see us through all of our seasons and love us unconditionally. Relationships with others teach us some of our greatest lessons.

At our core we want to be loved and we are worthy of being loved. When we do things from a place of love, we are love embodied. So, when we love ourselves, we allow others to love us for who we truly are – not the version we pretend to be around them.

What happens when you feel like you've fully stepped into loving yourself and you still aren't attracting the friendships or the romantic relationships you desire? I don't have all of the answers, but I'd like to share a few pieces from my experience that have helped me.

A few theories that have helped me over the years in regards to friendships:

- I am not participating in the hobbies or activities that I truly desire for this stage of my life. Therefore, I am not meeting friends that are meant to be in my life at this stage.
- I am doing the same things I've always done. *If we want to meet new people, we have to go to new places, try new things, or attend new events.*
- I have more work to do on accepting where I am now. I need to shift my focus to loving myself for exactly where I am, instead of always looking to the future.

A few theories that have helped me over the years in regards to romantic relationships:

- I am not attracting the right partner because I'm not at the equal level of where I desire them to be. I want to teach as much as I am taught.
- My partner has a lesson still to learn. I am ready, but they are not. They are on their own journey. Even though it feels like I am not meeting anyone, maybe it's because they are not ready for me yet.
- I need to get clear on what I actually want for myself and within a partnership.

Lately, I've been in a stage of life where I am single and surrounded by my closest friends getting married and starting families. The feelings of isolation that surround these seasons are truly heartbreaking at times.

From an earlier journal entry:
I'm so tired of being alone and I don't know
how to change that.
No one teaches you how to be alone.
No one teaches you how to be okay with
yourself in the quiet moments.

So much of society teaches us to find a partner to do life with. But what happens when that relationship ends or that person is no longer there? Or if you haven't found "the one" yet?

In my experience, too many people settle to check that box and not enough people embrace the opportunity to experience being single for a moment. To take the opportunity to fall in love with yourself and all that you can learn. Over the years, being single in a world full of couples has taught me a lot. And to be honest it is a roller coaster of equal parts self-love and self-pity.

> *"Some days I'm miserable about it. I'm so lonely and disappointed. I question what is wrong with me? Am I not loveable? When will I meet "the one"? But on the good days, I know it will happen when it's meant to happen. Either there is something more I need to learn or a lesson he hasn't learned yet. We're growing and evolving individually so that when we do meet, we will know. We will trust the timing of our relationship and the magic of how it is all happening exactly as it should be. We are waiting for the other to be ready for a fairytale. Because I will not settle for a mediocre life. Right now, as hard as it is some days, I know that I am building a strong foundation for my next relationship. The house I'm building is going to be secure. Full of love, laughter, trust and so much passion."* Ruth Montgomery, Journal Entry

> *"Feeling like I'm the only one I know not getting married and having kids. And I know the love I'm going to find is going to be so powerful and so worth it. But being isolated and different, no matter the circumstances never gets easy. We always, on some level, want to fit in."* Ruth Montgomery, Journal Entry

If you are single at the moment, then this is the perfect time to re-introduce yourself to yourself. One of the best things you can do if you find yourself here, is to take some time alone and find your independence again. Independent of who you are projecting onto the world, and independent of who you feel you have to show up as.

If you are solo, welcome. I have been here before, and solo in your 20s looks completely different than in your 30s when all of your friends are starting to get married and have kids. And I'm sure it's different again in your 40s, 50s, and so on. It's okay to be single. Some days it feels amazing, even liberating and other days it is gut-wrenching and terrifying. But it's okay. There is nothing wrong with being single in your adult life.

This journey of finding yourself or finding love feels like a roller coaster. From the highest moments celebrating that you are the only one responsible for your schedule and you can take all the 'me' time you desire. To the tiredness that comes from feeling like you're in this alone. The pain of loneliness and being alone is real. Here are some examples of my journal entries over the years, in and out of being single on my journey to finding love:

> *"What do I want to feel? I want to feel loved. I am ready for true, all-consuming love. The love of someone who understands, relates and pushes my soul. I want a dreamer – someone who can keep me grounded without limiting my dreams. I want to feel loved by a man who makes me feel beautiful, sexy and intelligent. Someone who is proud of me and someone I can be proud of. I want a relationship that is equal and adventurous – I want a fairytale. I am ready."* March 2018

> *"I am ready to be loved fully and completely. I am open to meeting someone who compliments my lifestyle, supports my dreams and is excited to grow with me as a person and as a couple."* December 2018

> *"I'm so excited for the days when I'll come home to my love. Be embraced and acknowledged just for being me. To create a life together where we both have our independent projects but can also collaborate and support each other as we succeed and through trying times. Our home will be full of love. A love so contagious, people will feel it as they enter our home."* July 2019

"I'm just really feeling the loneliness of being alone. What is wrong with me that I can't find someone? I'm so tired of being alone and I don't know how to change that. No one teaches you how to be okay by yourself in the quiet moments. Men wake up. We are ready for you. Ready to grow with you and to love. What is wrong with me? Why do I think anything is wrong with me? I just want to numb the pain. I don't want to feel. I don't want..."
August 2019

"The pain of being single is a lot of wtf am I doing? How am I not with anyone? Why is everyone else paired up? Yet so much of me knows it's happening now, it needs to. Either he's been learning something or I've needed to. We've been growing individually so that when we come together the magic will be more intense. More passionate. We will not settle for a mediocre life. When I see people communicate poorly or struggle to understand each other because they don't know themselves, I know that I am building a stronger foundation for my future relationship. The house I am building is going to be secure. Full of love, laughter and so much passion. But the pain of being alone in the moment is heart-breaking. It feels like isolation and abandonment. Makes you question everything. I desire passion. I desire purpose driven love. I desire a deep soul connection love. I desire finding oneness in myself and with a partner. He will not complete me, because I am whole. He will compliment me, because I can always learn more. Together we will love each other fiercely, passionately, truly, wholly, spiritually, magically – the stuff of a fairytale. They will believe in the magic of finding yourself to grow your love." November 2019

When we are single, or lacking in the quality of friendships we desire, it's easy to feel broken. Like something is wrong with us. Part of discovering who we truly are in order to find connections that truly feels good means we have to discover the truth of who we are. We have to go back to our core of what and who we desire in and for our lives. Who are we when we are alone?

You are whole. You have a whole heart. It's may have been mended a few times, but it's yours. Let it radiate within, outwardly and let the vibration mingle with other hearts. Let your heart be seen in its purity. Without fear of being hurt, for you know it is whole. Love is meant to enhance your heart; to amplify it. Not to feel like you've given part of it away. When you find partnerships or relationships that exemplify that, you know you're in the right space.

In 1957, a group of monks were being relocated due to the construction of a highway in Thailand. There was a monumental clay statue of Buddha that they wanted to preserve. It was so large though, that it started to crack when they tried to transport it. As it started to crack, it started to glisten from within. Upon discovering it, they realized that it was actually a golden Buddha that had been covered with clay. The monks discovered that previously the town had been invaded and they feared the Buddha would be ruined. They covered it with clay to disguise it, to decrease its value from the intruders. It remained unharmed for years, and the original Buddha was unknown to the new monks.

The moral of the story of the Golden Buddha is that we all have a golden Buddha within us, underneath our shell that we have built to keep us safe from the world. Much like the Buddha being relocated, it often takes some discomfort to discover our golden Buddha. We don't know what's within us, until we try something new, until we test the limits of our comfort zone. When we aren't finding relationships that align, it's often because we're staying within a comfort zone that we no longer desire to be in. We often have to take the leap, jumping into the abyss, and trusting that our wings will grow on the way down.

At the root of all of this, in knowing which leap to take, we have to learn to love ourselves for all that we are, as we are currently.

Each relationship you have offers you lessons in growth. Each partner you are with offers a different insight into what love can look like. It's important to honour your journey *and* honour their journey. To trust that wherever you are in your relationships right now, that you are exactly where you are supposed to be.

If you are currently in a relationship, know that you can start to learn more about yourself while still in a relationship. I would encourage you to get your partner to do the same.

Learning your love languages is a great way to amplify your connection. We each receive love differently, and Gary Chapman writes in his book, *The 5 Love Languages*, that the main ways we feel love are Quality Time, Words of Affirmation, Acts of Service, Giving Gifts, & Physical Touch. When we feel love, we often try to express love in the same way that we want to receive love, and that doesn't always work. For instance, if your love language is words of affirmation, and you are constantly complimenting your partner as your rush off to your next event thinking you are giving love. When in reality they prefer quality time, all they notice is that you're always rushing from one place to the next. We give and receive love differently. It's just as important to find out how the people in your life receive love so that you can show them how much they mean to you in a language they understand.

An Extra Dose of Magic
To find out your love language, take Gary Chapman's quiz here:
5lovelanguages.com/quizzes/love-language

Finding Yourself as Your Relationships Evolve

When I was in high school, I had two pet turtles, and I was told that turtles will only grow as big as their environment allows. This has always stuck with me because I see it in people constantly. You will only grow as big as your environment allows. Be that the mentality of the town you live in, the friendships you maintain, the relationships you choose or the jobs you stay in. For example, have you ever felt alone, when you're lying next to the person who's supposed to love you the most? Have you ever been in a job that you know doesn't align anymore, but you find excuses to stay even though you feel like no one understands you? What about a friendship that feels like you're repeating the same conversations every weekend – on an endless loop going nowhere?

We've all been there. And what I've learned from these situations, is that it is time to change your environment. Maybe you're not ready to physically change your environment, but mentally you can start to change your internal environment. By dating yourself, you can start to tap back into who you are, and what you want for yourself. Eventually, the people around you will start to adapt. Or you'll get so exhausted from your situation, you'll have the courage to change your physical environment.

Remember that you are enough; in all that you are, in all that you are learning and in all that you are becoming. We go through cycles of feeling like too much or not enough. The truth is you are perfect. *And* like anything there are ebbs and flows.

When you are feeling like too much, be the light others wish they had in themselves. Shine in your light to allow others to step up into theirs. Show them what's possible.

And when you are feeling like not enough, remember your story is important. You matter and you are needed here. You are enough.

Trust The Process

Nature is a great reminder to put full trust into the process. I think of butterflies when I think of all of the messy gooey lessons we go through. Do you think caterpillars know they haven't reached their full potential when they are still a caterpillar? Do you think they know it's their destiny to become a butterfly? That the stage of a caterpillar is only the beginning? Think about it, they are fairly helpless as a caterpillar, and life moves pretty slowly. Day after day, finding food and trying to survive.

Next, they go into a cocoon – does this feel like rock bottom? Do they feel like they will never come out of this alive? Or that life is over, because it's so hard, and they just can't see what's coming next? It's gooey and messy and dark. Or do they feel like this is a hibernation, and they are going through some tough changes to become a better version of themselves? Do they recognize this as self-development as they are in the cocoon state?

As they emerge as a butterfly, they are the most beautiful version of themselves. Not necessarily just in physical looks, but because they have the confidence to fly. They are exploring new territory and at new heights (literally).

Like all things in life, the chaos comes before the beauty can emerge. The tornado has to disrupt nature in order for it to rebuild. The caterpillar has to go into her cocoon before she can spread her wings as a butterfly. This may sound corny, but it's so beautifully true. Perhaps our beauty and strength come after the struggle. Perhaps we all need the chaos to recognize how beautiful life is.

You are the only you. You are here for a purpose and more importantly, on purpose. Let the world see you, let them find you and let them love you.

It's all a part of trusting the process. Trust that what you are going through will teach you something. Or the path that maybe doesn't make sense in the moment, will end up being a crucial piece to your story unfolding.

"In one year from now, I won't even know who this version of me is. This is the year of stepping into me. My truly authentic purpose with passion and integrity. There are bound to be lessons, but the triumphs and growth will far out shine those. I will allow the space to still create and explore. I will be present in the moment. Learning to be here and in the now. To be fully me and to embrace each version of me. To be love, to be loved and to love."

Ruth Montgomery, Journal Entry

It's time to jump into the abyss, metaphorically speaking! It's time to trust that your wings will grow as you freefall. Leap and learn to fly trusting that you are fully supported in this journey!

PHASE THREE

ACCEPTANCE

Acceptance.

What does this really mean?

To fully accept yourself means to not simply give in and let it be what it is, but to embrace and accept all pieces of yourself. To start to see yourself fully, without judgement, for all that you are. To learn to love and accept each piece of that.

Acceptance, here, within yourself, means to see the good and the bad in equal balance. We have so many pieces of ourselves and if we didn't have the negative aspects, we wouldn't fully appreciate the positive aspects.

However, in order to accept ourselves, we must first understand. This is *the work*; understanding and accepting yourself. From where you came from, to who you are becoming and everything in between.

Accepting yourself from a place of understanding – for all that you are.

Shadow Self

Shadow Work has this mysterious charm about it. It feels big, and powerful, yet exclusive only to those worthy of doing "the work". In the most basic of terms, Shadow Work is recognizing and bringing awareness to your shadows. Seeing your shadow self, and bringing that part into the light. Your shadow self is created by the pieces of yourself that you keep hidden. This could be in the moments that you maybe regret or the actions and words you wish you could undo. It might be the character traits that you keep repeating, even though they make you feel like shit. It's found in the things you don't love about yourself and the patterns you see, but can't seem to stop. It's the traits or stories we tell ourselves that have a more negative connotation to them. Your shadows are, simply, the pieces that need to be brought into the light. Bringing them into the light transforms them so you can co-exist with them as a positive essence.

That's the shadow work. Because as soon as you bring light to those pieces of yourself, the darkness loses all power. Have you ever had a secret that you've held onto so tightly, it's kept you up at night? And then as soon as you spoke it out loud, it suddenly lost all power because it was out in the world?

The things we fear the most, are often the things that keep us playing small. We don't want someone else to see the things about us that we dislike the most.

Have you ever been in a relationship that's ending or not going so well, where your partner starts to call out the parts of yourself you dislike? Or the bully on the school yard that pokes fun at the "flaws" you so desperately hoped no one else noticed? It cuts so deep, because we have barely acknowledged those pieces of ourselves.

From my experience, this also works in reverse. I know I am falling out of love with someone, when I start to pick at their flaws. It's a low blow, I know. Yet it's an easy way for the ego to step in to start to acknowledge that we are done here. It's interesting when you start to see it, because earlier in your relationship, it was maybe those quirks you loved most about them. What a hurtful transition. It is absolutely a defense mechanism as our shadow self fears being seen. Unfortunately, we stoop to that lower vibrational energy, to call out their shadows, before they can call out ours. This is coming from a place of fear, instead of acceptance.

Imagine, as a teenager what would have happened if we were taught that our imperfections were actually the qualities that set us apart. The body features that we don't love because they are "different", often turn out to be the pieces we love most about ourselves as adults. The traits we get criticized for can, in the right light, become our brightest power. Imagine, if we learned to love those shadow pieces of ourselves, we could also learn to love (and ultimately accept) the shadow pieces of others, unconditionally and without judgement.

This is the polarity between the light and the dark. Being aware and awake to it all, gives *you* the power back.

> "I see that my understanding of the darkness gives
> my search for the light context and meaning."

Brené Brown, Gifts of Imperfections

What in yourself, do you secretly hope that no one notices? What do you hide or cover-up? What feels like you could release the weight off of your shoulders if you simply spoke it out loud? Trust, whatever comes to mind. Our mind, although it sometimes feels like it deceives us, truly speaks from the soul and wants the best for us. It's in the split second that we second guess ourselves that our ego gets the chance to step in.

So, listen. What came first? What thought or memory do you need to bring into the light? And what would that look like? Do you need to journal about it, speak it out loud to yourself in the mirror, or tell someone you love? What weighs heavy on your heart?

"But in truth you are not your heart.
You are the experiencer of your heart."

Michael Singer, The Untethered Soul

You are not your shadow. You are not your darkness. You are experiencing these pieces of yourself to bring yourself more fully into the light; to elevate and evolve as you step more into yourself.

Shadow work feels like such a daunting piece of "the work", yet it truly can be so simple. It's what you uncover about yourself when you reveal your shadows that is the hard part. Taking time to see the parts of ourselves is one of the simplest things we can do, with the greatest impact.

Bringing in Support

Recognizing and bringing awareness to your shadows while being willing to sit and acknowledge the dark pieces of yourself can feel heavy. This is a reminder that you do not have to do this alone. There are many modalities in which you can use to support you through this. Not all require an exchange of energy, but from my experience, the quickest way to work with your shadows is to hire someone to hold space for you while you move through it. Bringing in unbiased support, in the forms of a therapist, energy healer, or coach who is trained in holding space for this type of work can help ease the process.

Hiring a professional can allow you to face the parts of yourself you don't necessarily love with less room for judgement. Unlike, with a friend or family member, this person has not been personally affected by your shadows. This is beneficial for two main reasons.

One – they have the skill set and understanding of how complex shadow work can be. In the instance where this stems from a past trauma, they have the skills to help you through it, without causing more harm. Obviously, this is extremely important. We want to be able to identify and either unpack or shift the shadow, not make the shadow bigger or give it more power.

Two – they are unbiased. Meaning this doesn't allow someone else's feelings to be brought into play. When talking through shadow work with family or friends, it can often cause more confusion. If the other person was a part of or has experienced this shadow piece of yourself, they may be remembering where it affected them. This can be reflected back to you, adding more shame, or embarrassment. If you are in a vulnerable state trying to heal this, and someone places blame on you, it's easy to shut down and shove the shadow back into its depths. Because hiding it, and pretending it never happened, is easier than facing it in the short term. Sharing with a family member or friend, as you are healing, can also lead to opening up their own wounds where they share a similar shadow. This *can* be very healing; however, we have to be sensitive to this. If you are also trying to heal this, you may not have the space to support them as well as yourself – in which case it can be more harmful than helpful.

Taking Pause

This is ongoing work. This is never-ending, *if you choose*. The reminder here is that you have a choice. It's your life. It's *your* soul's journey. You can and *must* take breaks when you are called to. Look for signs of burnout or overwhelm, and allow yourself to pause. With each layer, you may uncover different truths that also need time to process and accept.

This pause is where the transformation happens. The first step is definitely awareness, but the magic happens when you can alchemize your shadows into the light. In between these steps is often a pause.

Most of us have been taught to be busy all of our lives. To accomplish, to do and to check things off your list – rarely to be. Think of these pauses like your cocoon phase. You once were a caterpillar, and in order to become a butterfly, you must take pause in your cocoon as you transform. These pauses allow you to come out the other side bigger and better than ever before, with more clarity and in better alignment with yourself. These pauses allow you to see and embrace your unique magic.

"I am like a butterfly in her cocoon patiently waiting to spread my wings. Long overdue for this pause. Absorbing the richness of what life has taught me so far, allowing myself to be guided by my awareness and inner knowing. Reflecting on all that has come before this moment. Ready to magically step into the next version of radiance. Excited to soar."

Ruth Montgomery, Journal Entry

This pause gives us a chance to reflect on how far we've come, on the stories that we have previously told ourselves and how we want to proceed moving forward. It is important to take the time to collect our thoughts, to understand where this has come from in the past, and to decide whether it is still serving us or not. Sometimes, there will be pieces of ourselves that we're not ready to process. Some are still serving to protect parts of ourselves that aren't ready to be healed yet. These pauses, much like a cocoon can be messy and filled with goo as we literally shed layers and versions of ourselves.

Along this journey of personal development, different seeds will be planted. Some will make sense right away and others will take time for your body and soul to catch up. This is true with shadow work as well. It can start as an uncomfortable emotion, perhaps a comment or situation that triggers you and you aren't quite sure why. Knowing in your body that it means more than meets the eye, but unsure what it means. Something else may bring up that same feeling days, months or even years later. It's like connecting the dots until you can see the full picture.

When you can almost see the full picture, enough to know what image will appear, it is important to keep going. Finish connecting the dots so that you can colour in the image with bright colours as you accept and alchemize your shadows. Remembering that this life is *your* connect the dots. Some of the numbers or steps will blur together because they come is such quick succession. Others will have pauses in between; take as long as you need at each particular stage to embody or to rest. This isn't a competition – it's simply a beautiful journey!

Bringing Your Shadows Into Light

Self-awareness around where your blocks are or where shame or fear lives for you, is the first step, because we cannot heal what we are not aware of.

Awareness allows us to alchemize the perceived negative connotation into a positive acceptance. This may require a change in perspective, an understanding of the root of origination, a release of the stories no longer serving you or a realization that we all have shadows.

Shadows can show up in things such as; selfishness, judgement, shame, need to control, temper tantrums, cockiness, and so on. For each of these examples, ask yourself, where does this show up in my life? Or use the journal prompts provided at the back of the book for a further deep-dive.

I find journaling to be one of the best ways to really see what your body and soul is trying to tell you. This is a great tool to use situationally as something triggers you, or you have uncomfortable feelings come up. Writing down and acknowledging your experience allows you to bring awareness to your shadows.

Moving *Through* Your Shadows

Now that we can recognize where there is perhaps more to discover, we can start to move through our shadows. Simply asking, where is this coming from? Why am I responding this way? (Either by speaking out loud or journaling).

This is an important stage. When we acknowledge our shadows, we create awareness. But without further diving into them, they maintain their power of being a shadow – as something worthy of fearing.

Think about walking through a forest, on a bright sunny day. The sun streaming through the trees, highlighting the beauty of the leaves. A slight wind blows through, feeling the warmth on your face, and the refreshing feeling as the wind catches your hair or your jacket. The sounds of birds chirping – cheerfully talking to each other. The babbling brook in the distance, offering a calm sensation of how connected this world is. How beautifully tranquil.

Now picture that same forest on a cold misty night. The wind whistling through the trees, the sounds of unknown animals reminding you you're not alone here. The chills that run through your body as you navigate the dark ground, nervous where you step because you can't see what's in front of you.

Two completely different experiences, same forest. Our shadows hold the power over us, much like a dark shadowy forest. And that fear loses its power when day breaks and you can see clearly again.

If we choose not to move through our shadows, honouring what emotions come up and experiencing the emotions they offer, they stay shadows. We will continually be shown those shadows until we're ready to face them.

Moving through our shadows can look like sitting with them, feeling the emotions that come up, experiencing the full depth of emotions they offer, speaking about them, and understanding where they came from. Allowing yourself to experience them for all that they are, without judgement or embarrassment. Honouring them for all that they are here to teach you.

Alchemizing Shadows

Lovingly allow yourself to re-frame your flaws or triggers and allow yourself to be perfectly imperfect. This is an ongoing lesson for most of us, because as we grow spiritually and soulfully, we encounter new levels. As the saying goes, "new levels, new devils". Each evolution of ourselves will uncover new lessons in self-development.

Let's start with an easy introduction: take the negative self-talk and make a list of your "flaws" or character traits that you dislike. The things you dislike about yourself, and the things that trigger you when others say them about you. (I say "flaws" but I don't believe we have flaws. I believe we have qualities that offer a lot of insight into who we are. It is these qualities that make us unique, and for that I refuse to see them as negative.)

Now, it's time to re-frame those words and dive deeper into their perceived power. Ask yourself, why do you understand those words as negative flaws, when they have the power to be positive character traits?

Often as children we have different labels that get attached to us. As adults, they can trigger an uncomfortable feeling. For instance, as a child I was called "bossy". I was an only child until I was 7 years old, and had a stubborn streak from the age of 3. I knew what I wanted, and I went about getting what I wanted the only way I knew how to as a child. Bossy by definition is an adjective describing someone as "given to ordering people about". Some of the synonyms of bossy are imperious, pushy, commanding, and strict. Bossy can be perceived as a negative flaw absolutely. As a quality to be embraced, bossy can translate into someone who is confident, decisive and a born leader (also known as, a boss). When we look at a "Boss", as a title, we see it as a position of authority, generally deserving respect. "Bossy", as a character trait can be over-domineering and controlling, often frowned upon. All of this can dive deeper into our patriarchy programing, as growing up, typically a "Boss" was male, and a woman exemplifying the same qualities was labelled "bossy", like it's a bad thing. This is where you get to determine what resonates with you and whether you still believe it to be true about yourself.

Diving into the actual definitions of the words and labels is a powerful place to start. Words are important, and we often unknowingly attach different meanings to them. Start by defining your labels yourself. What do they mean to you? Next, look up the word in the dictionary to truly understand the definition, and find the synonyms of that word. Keep playing off of those words until you find one you like. One that alchemizes the word from a preconceived negative label to an empowering one! A few other examples to consider as you dive into your own words are:

Indecisive, can also be described as cautious or thoughtful.

Weird, can also translate into unique, one of a kind or extraordinary.

Another powerful exercise is to examine why these words trigger you. For example, when you are being "indecisive" is it because you really want to be making the decision you need to make? Who says you really have to make that decision anyways? Often traits like this are because we are forcing ourselves to do something that isn't in the right time or it's not the right place. Allow yourself the time and grace to step back and re-evaluate why. This can show up as your soul recognizing that this is a decision you don't actually want to make, but something that someone else perhaps told you, you should or had to.

Consider where you were first told these words were flawed. Does it come from a childhood memory? For example, were you constantly told you were weird as a child? Does it come from a situational experience? Did you get left out of a group activity as a kid because you were "weird"? And now you associate being left out from being weird? *Or* do you subconsciously exclude yourself because you've convinced yourself that you are weird and that's what happens to weird people? Can you step back and examine when you first decided to believe the negativity about yourself?

Noticing what memories come up, we can look at it as an adult now and see it from a whole new perspective. Put yourself in your shoes as a child and acknowledge how it must have felt in the moment. Now that you are older, and not immediately in the situation, you can also look at the circumstances of the event – what were the other people going through? How were they projecting their own hurt onto you? We can see these characters with love now, and honour that everyone was on their own journey.

Only you get to decide if you are going to live by these words and continue to let them define you. By allowing them to bother you, you are giving those words power. And in turn giving those people who call you those words power over you.

An Extra Dose of Magic

If this is an overwhelming exercise, I would recommend you seek someone to hold space for you as you do this. Find a mentor or a coach that can sit with you without judgement and let you talk through these. Or seek a health professional. Psychotherapists are amazing and I highly recommend finding someone of that calibre to work through any negative self-talk like this. There are some incredible healers and confidence coaches out there too. Healers and guides are here to guide you to heal yourself. They will not heal you. You are a healer, you have to be willing to do the work, and allow them to guide you in your magic, to find your healing.

When hiring anyone to do this work, trust how you feel. Do you get a good gut feeling or does it feel like something is off? Listen to your body. You know. You will be guided to the right people.

Once you have reframed or accepted these so-called flaws as positive attributes - you cut off their power and you stop giving others permission to use them against you. So next time, someone calls you weird, you can own it, "Actually I am unique, so if that's weird to you, then yes I am weird and I love it."

Once you have reframed these traits, know that the people who judge you, are often judging themselves first. For example, there's probably a part of them that wishes they could let their weird quirks show. It is easier to place judgement on someone else, than it is to look within to exam what we don't like about ourselves.

It also comes back to perception. How do you know what that other person is really thinking about you when they call you a word that triggers you? Do you know for a fact, that the person calling you that so-called-flaw is perceiving it as a negative trait? Or is that your internal perception of it? If that's the case, you can ask them to explain what they mean when they call you a certain word. Have them explain their understanding of it, or what they are really trying to say. Often, we use words as placeholders for a much deeper meaning.

With all of these shadows, the goal is not necessarily to change them within you, but to understand how they are interpreted within you. To become aware of them and to see them in a different light, ultimately to detach from them. Naturally as you become more aware of your shadows, you will start to transform and release the stories and behaviours that are no longer serving you as you evolve. For example, hiding your "weirdness" is a story to keep you playing small out of fear of being seen. When you can own that your weirdness is your uniqueness, you stand out and shine. There comes a point in each of our lives, where we get over our own self-limiting beliefs – sometimes a simple re-frame is all it takes.

Shadows can also show up in situations where we are passing judgement or trying to over control a situation. When we are judging others, it's often reflecting something in us, that we either don't love or something that we wish we had. When we try to control situations, it's often because we sense a lack of control within our own lives and we start to grasp control over the people and events around us. Our behaviour is always a reflection of ourselves.

Ongoing Shadows

With each layer that we uncover, there will always be more. This is not a one and done process. Each shadow will take as long as it needs, often depending on how deeply tied to your identity it is, or how much it has impacted you. It does get easier though. What used to take weeks or even months to process, can now take hours or days for me to move through the emotions. The more you start to connect to your soul, the less fight the ego puts up to release what is no longer serving you.

As you evolve, more and more shadows will appear. You'll start to connect the dots to pieces of your life you would've never thought possible to connect. And you'll start to understand yourself on a whole new level. It can be uncomfortable, but I want to remind you how beautiful it gets to be.

It's like the caterpillar going into its cocoon – that's often what this feels like. It feels like we're stumbling around in the dark, knowing there must be a light, but we can't find the switch right away. You are a butterfly, and you will create the light. Keep going, and don't be afraid to pause when needed and ask for support when things feel heavy.

Unlearning

We are constantly told to seek more, especially through consumerism, and through our current education system. From day one, we are instilled with the idea that *more* equals *better*. The belief that we are not enough is a constant throughout our lives. You'll get the job you love, *when* you have more experience. You'll make more money, *if* you have more education. You'll be happier, *when* you have more things in your home. Constantly we are told to add to our lives. To aspire to have, do and be *more*.

The real learning however, is in the *un*learning. When we start to strip back the layers of who we think we are and of who we thought we wanted to be. We have to unbecome who we once were, to become who we are meant to be.

There are so many layers to unlearning. In this work, just when you thought you had experienced it all, and uncovered who you are, there is another layer. In the unlearning, you can go as deep as you want. Knowing that this work is a choice, and if at any point you need to pause in a layer, then pause. You have full permission to do this work at whatever speed feels good for you.

The unlearning requires us to look at our habits and our beliefs. It's important to decipher, what is learned and what is ours. What belongs to you, and what is no longer working for you? Throughout this section, remember that this is a constant re-evaluation. What once worked successfully for you, doesn't have to continue to work for you for the rest of your life. And if it is still successfully working for you, keep doing it! The point is you have permission to question and re-evaluate everything. You get to choose what you want to change and what you want to keep; be it your opinion, your beliefs, your habits, or your surroundings. You can change your mind, whenever you choose.

The world as we know it, is only as we know it because of what we know. *Take a minute and read that again.* You only know what you know. And you don't know what you don't know. So, what you perceive the world as, is only as you know it.

There are so many takes on how the world works. And my reality will be different than your reality because of our upbringings, because of the people we've been surrounded by and by the people we choose to surround ourselves with. As an individual you learn from everyone you meet, and if you allow it, you take on other people's perceptions to make up your own perception of the world.

When was the last time you stepped back from the beliefs you've been given and actually evaluated what beliefs are yours? How much of what you believe is what your parents believe? Or your friends believe? How much of what you believe became a belief in order to fit in?

Our beliefs have to start from somewhere, and as mentioned earlier, I believe our souls choose our parents. Some part of you chose to believe how they see the world, because on some level those beliefs served you. Either to allow you to stand strongly in your own beliefs because they are valued and true to you. Or because you desired to break free from that belief system and your soul needed to have empathy with those beliefs to pursue something greater.

After your initial upbringing, you start to have some conscious choice in who you surround yourself with. Some of these people will have very strong views on the world; whether it be on global topics such as politics, social injustice, gender normality, historical views, climate change, or healthcare. Perhaps on more personal topics such as what is fashionable, what is healthy for our bodies to ingest, how to interact with money and how we respect the people around us. These ideas that you are around will influence how you speak and act. As we are learning who we are, it's easy to go with the flow of agreement and acceptance. It's easier to accept these beliefs as truth than to question the people you love and respect.

Have you ever had that nagging, unsettled feeling when someone is speaking about what they believe? Or it makes you embarrassed or uncomfortable to hear and you want to change the subject? This is your soul's way of suggesting it is time you re-frame your thinking. Your soul is guiding you to feel uncomfortable, to physically feel that "gut reaction" in your body to know that something is off.

It's okay to question the people around you. It's okay to do your own research and find out what other people believe. Listen to podcasts, watch documentaries, use the internet, join different social groups, and start having conversations with people outside of your "normal".

My dad always taught me, there are three sides to every story. Your side of the story, my side of the story and the truth of what actually happened. None will match completely, and we will never know how all three truly fit together. Expanding on this there are three versions of truth in any belief system. There is *your* truth, there is *my* truth and there is *the* truth. All valuable. All equal in their standing. All can co-exist together. None, more correct than the others. Yet each is different based on what you know, and what your lived experience has been.

It is not about convincing others to believe what you believe, but about opening up to understanding where their perception has led them. And to understand that they may empathize with different aspects of the world due to their upbringing and the people they know.

You only know what you know. And you don't know what you don't know. Take the time to get to know some of what you don't know. Take the time to get to know yourself. To know and understand why you believe what you believe. Who or what has shaped your ideas? Are you holding onto someone else's perceived perception of you?

It's okay if your truth or your beliefs change, as you change. What you once believed to be true (with the information you had at the time) may no longer resonate with you. What can happen, is we get so attached to our beliefs that we forget to check in and see if they still resonate. Change can be hard, and our ego doesn't like it. Our ego will hold on so tightly to your past believes because it's comfortable, not necessarily because it serves you anymore. This is where the magic happens – where we can get curious about our lives, about our story and our beliefs.

Habits & Behaviours

Let's start at the surface, what do you do in your daily life that no longer resonates with you? Take an inventory of your day, write down a few things you did today. Here's a couple examples from my morning:

1. I woke up with no alarm when my body was ready.
2. I went and got groceries without a list, asking my body what I needed in that moment.
3. I came home to write and made myself a coffee.

Okay, seems mundane, but let's break this down.

1. I woke up with no alarm when my body was ready.

For years, (I am 33 years old writing this), I woke up to an alarm - feeling like I had to jump out of bed, and start my day. It felt like I had to be productive from the moment I woke up. When I started working for myself, I was living in this narrative that I had to work from 9am until 4 or 5pm. I struggled for months to get out of bed, and be working by 9am. Often I found I was working until 8 or 9pm at night. My body was so productive in the evenings, yet, every day I still forced myself to get out of bed and "start" my day at 9am. While working with my coach at the time, I told her I was struggling. I had been re-writing my to-do list every day that week – I had a bit of a cold and could not seem to focus. She asked me what absolutely had to be done that day. Honestly? Nothing, all of it could wait. In that moment, she gave me permission to take the rest of the day off.

191

Guilt-free – to rest, and relax and give my body the time it needed. I woke up the next day excited to start my day, and I got everything done on my to-do list that day that I had been "working" on all week. It was in that moment, that I realized I was living my week out of alignment. I chose to start my own business so I didn't have to work a 9-5. Yet, here I was still trying to fit the mold of a 9-5, unsuccessfully and getting so frustrated with myself for not making it work. It wasn't me that wasn't working – it was the system I was trying to fit into.

The deeper layer to this is that when I was a child, I missed the bus constantly because I slept in – what felt like a couple times a week, my mum had to drive me to school. She would get so frustrated with me, because on Saturday mornings, I would be up at 6am all on my own to watch Saturday morning cartoons. The more I reflected on this, another part of my childhood memories started to surface; something I've always known, but honestly thought nothing of, because it just was what it was. My dad always left the house first in the morning, and he somewhere along the way, decided that we all needed to be up when he left. What I'm sure started as a gentle morning reminder the first time he tried to wake us up, ended up turning into a frustrated "it's time to get up" awakening by his third or fourth attempt.

As an adult now, I can see why he would be frustrated if he had spoken to us in our sleepy states three-four times, and we still weren't listening. I would be frustrated too. But as the child, who slept through the first one-two gentle reminders, I was being awoken to the frustrated version of that. Starting my day off with a loud, rude awakening. (Much like an alarm jolting you out of sleep). When I sat with this, my body remembers that, and that frustration from my dad, was how I was starting my day, feeling jolted and confused. Now, as an adult, of course that's what my body reverts to when an alarm rudely wakes me up. I'm agitated and slightly annoyed, even though I set that alarm. I was in this cycle of starting my day irritated.

Acknowledging where the pattern began and why it is out of alignment for me now, is the first step in starting to understand and accept where we are. Because without first accepting where you are, you cannot change the outcome.

Through discovering this, I have realized that I thrive when my mornings start out slowly – much like my 6am Saturday morning cartoons. I like to wake up when my body desires, and I love to lay in bed, or cuddled up in a cozy chair with a hot cup of coffee. Sometimes, just sitting with my thoughts, staring out the window, or journaling. Once I got into a bit of a routine, my body generally gets up around 6 or 7am depending on the season. I have learned that I like about 2-3 hours to get ready in the morning to be able to take that time to just sit and be without feeling rushed. Knowing this, I started operating my business this way, not accepting any meetings or client calls until at least 10am. That way I know, every day I can wake up without stressing that I need to be anywhere, or that I've missed an appointment. Obviously, there are some exceptions, but generally speaking this is how I operate.

This is something I check in with often, and it will shift every few months depending on what I am working on, and what time of year it is. I know not everyone has the luxury of 3 hours in the morning to get ready, but for me that's where my priorities were in this season. I think it's important to remember too, that your priorities can also be re-evaluated every once in a while. If you find you desire slow mornings as well, and "can't seem to find the time". Look at where else you are spending your time? Are you watching three hours of television in the evenings? What would happen if you went to bed earlier, and cut out the television in the evening so you could have the three hours in the morning? It's not always so simple, I know, sometimes it just takes a bit of creativity to "find the time".

2. I went and got groceries without a list, asking my body what I needed in that moment.

Do you remember when you first went grocery shopping by yourself? Did you automatically know what to buy? Or did you look to see what other people were buying? Did you resort to what your parents had always bought and the labels that were familiar? We're never really taught what to buy to prepare the meals that our body needs. We are taught through observations to eat what we know or what we think we're supposed to.

I remember when I first went to college, I thought I had to buy a lot of "college food" like peanut butter and kraft dinner, because that was the narrative - that in college, that's what you survived off of. When I was first living with a partner, and trying to make our own version of a home, we ate a lot of meat and potato type meals because that's what we always ate in our family homes. When I moved out on my own, there were days I didn't have a lot of money so I ate soup, and kraft dinner because it was easy and I didn't want to spend hundreds of dollars on groceries. I was resorting to the narrative that college students are poor (as seen on many televisions shows and movies), and when you are poor that's the type of food you eat – quick, easy, pre-packaged.

I love food. I have travelled all over the world, and one of my favourite things is to experience a delicious meal. I love it and I will prioritize it without a second thought, because I'm "on vacation". So why, when I'm at home, don't I cook delicious meals that bring me as much joy as when I'm on vacation? You can buy a lot of delicious items for a reasonable price, but the mentality is they are "expensive". It often costs less, but takes more time to create delicious meals (and meals with more nutritional value).

I have also told myself for years that I am not a cook. I don't cook. I don't enjoy cooking. In this last couple of years of living on my own, and doing this personal development work, I've learned that I actually do love to cook. That was simply a narrative I've been telling myself.

Cooking in my family, like many families I know, is just something you do with very little passion or enthusiasm. It's often a role the mother figure takes on. And when the family gets home, the mom is expected to have dinner on the table. Most families, like my own, cook what they know. They cook what their parents cooked; who cooked what their parents cooked.

There's a story about a family who traditionally cooks a pot roast every year for the family holiday meal. Every year they cut the pot roast in half and cook it in two halves. One year, a guest joined them for the meal and asked, why do you cut the pot roast in half? They looked around and no one knew why - they just always have. They finally asked the grandmother if she knew why, and she said of course! When she was younger their ovens were much smaller, so the roast had to be cut in half to fit in the oven. That's all. It didn't change the flavour or make it cook any better. It was so habitual, and expected, that no one had ever questioned *why* they cut it in half. How many things do we do like this, without really knowing why, that no longer serves us?

Deciding what to make for dinner is a chore in my family home. Day in, day out, it seems to be a decision that takes up so much time and energy. My mom will ask us what we want for dinner, after years of having the "obligation" to decide, that decision is now exhausting. Yet no one else wants to decide. Where does this idea come from? That the responsibility gets placed on one person to decide what to have, to prepare *and* cook the meal. It takes hours out of their day. I think for me, I saw this growing up, and how much resentment it brought with it. It made cooking feel like such a big undertaking. You have to decide what to eat, you have to accommodate for everyone else in the home, you have to buy the groceries, you have to do the prep work, and cook the meal. Only for everyone to sit down, and eat it quickly as they rush off to the next hockey game or meeting. Leaving someone responsible for dishes and cleanup, with next to zero appreciation for what goes into a meal in the chaos that is a busy family home. This is no judgment about the men in our lives, because they also are doing what they learned as "normal" behaviour.

That doesn't sound enjoyable at all, therefore, of course, I don't like cooking with that narrative running in the background of my subconscious.

Interestingly, going out to a restaurant, you take the time, to sit and enjoy the meal. And yes, someone else has to make the food, serve the food and do the clean-up. But as the person eating the meal, you get to decide what you eat. Isn't it crazy that at home, no one wants to make a decision around what to eat, yet at a restaurant, that is the excitement of getting to choose what you eat?

In reflecting on this, I generally do like cooking because I enjoy eating good food and the experience that goes along with that. What I do not like is the fast paced, eat without enjoyment, and lack of appreciation that comes with so many meals.

Over the years, I started trying to explore meals beyond meat and potatoes. I started to bring in more of the flavours and cuisines I loved from around the world. What I noticed was the food I was trying to make was new to the people I was eating it with. It was often out of their comfort zone, and instead of being recognized as *different*, it was acknowledged as *not good*.

The truth of the story was never that I wasn't a good cook – I'm sure there were a few not so great meals, I'm not denying that. But the food I was cooking was often different than then their normal, which I allowed to translate into a meaning that wasn't mine. I allowed that narrative, that the food wasn't good to directly mean I wasn't good at cooking.

So now, when I cook, I cook for me. And I enjoy cooking as an experience. I enjoy the time in the kitchen with a partner. Making a meal together, to enjoy it together. Obviously, not every meal has the time, so kraft dinner is still a great option once in a while, but now because I choose it, not because that's all I tell myself I can afford. I also choose different ingredients to try new cuisines or to experiment with new recipes.

Now, back to the grocery shopping today – when I am grocery shopping, I am able to ask my body what it desires, rather than just go to a default meal. Do I need more fruit or citrus today? Is my body craving bread and pasta? Do I need or desire meat today or more of a vegetarian meal?

I am not shopping from a place of what is familiar, or standard. I shop from a place of curiosity and desire. Money can still play into this yes, and this is a great opportunity to start to really dive into what your body craves. If, today, you can only afford one or the other, what is your body telling you it actually wants? I have gone grocery shopping for far too many years, buying salad greens only to throw it out untouched weeks later because I "should" eat a salad. No more of that. I buy what my body needs, and desires, not what I should eat based on what I've grown up thinking, or what the media or people around me are saying is "good" for me. Your body knows. Trust it.

3. I came home to write and made myself a coffee.

The piece of this I want to draw your attention to is the coffee. I had a coffee at 11am – the first coffee of my day. Did I need a coffee to start my day? No. Did I need a coffee to write? No. I chose to have a coffee, because I desired the warmth. The comfort that a cup of coffee brings.

Many of us, over time, have started to believe that we "need" coffee. It's a worldwide narrative, and a multi-billion-dollar industry. Just look at the line-ups at your local drive-through or coffee shop during the morning rush.

So, I ask you to consider, if you consume coffee every day, why do you drink coffee?

- Is it a belief that you *need* it to function?
- Is it an addiction – either the beverage or the habit?
- Is it a desire that you are fulfilling?

There are no wrong answers here, but I want you to take the time to simply ask the question. When was the last time you thought about why you drank coffee every day? Where did it start?

For a long time, I didn't like coffee, but I was addicted to Iced Cappuccinos from Tim Horton's. I loved them. I craved them. I couldn't go anywhere without getting one. I didn't need it; I desired it, and that desire became a habit. That habit became an addiction and suddenly I was buying at least one a day, telling myself that I needed it. When I was able to step back, and realize I didn't need it.

I recognized over time that I didn't even enjoy it anymore, so why was I continuing to spend so much money on something I didn't really like?

When I think about it, it was the habit of having something to drink while driving. Having something to occupy my hands, and a reason to stop and take a break from driving. And more than that, it was the habit of belonging, when everyone else was getting a coffee, the feeling of being included in the "coffee run". The feeling of belonging to a not-so-secret club. The feeling of fitting in. At the end of the day, isn't that what we all want? Isn't that what we're taught? To fit or to blend in.

When you think about it, isn't that the opposite of what our souls truly desire? Sure, we need community, and we need companions – we are not meant to do this life alone. But to fit in so much, that we lose ourselves? That's not the point.

Over time, I have switched my coffee preference to double doubles (two creams and two sugars). Regularly I will check in and ask myself, do I still want a double double? Or am I having this because this is my usual order. Try different flavours or options to see if what you're consuming is still what you desire most. And if yes, great. Carry on. If not, seek the opportunity to find a better suited option for the current version of yourself.

Choosing coffee today, was less about fitting in, and more about the choice my body desired. I wanted the warmth, and the comfort it offered. And yet perhaps still, on a deeper level, as I drink my coffee alone today, I desired that feeling of belonging from a distance, to the not-so-secret club. And all of this is okay, but I question it every once in a while, to make sure my habits are coming out of desire verses previous expectations.

Another great area to look at is your current bedtime routine. Does it resonate with you, and provide you with the support you need for who you are becoming? We focus on bedtime routines as children – reading a story before bed, brushing teeth, and lights out a certain time. Somewhere along the way we lose that. What you desired as a child or desire for your children (current, future or the future generation) is a great place to start if you're feeling lost. Go back to the basics.

Additionally, consider your habits when it comes to alcohol or other substances. Are your current behaviours serving you? Do they mimic what you grew up with or witnessed in your social group as the norm? What about your television viewing habits? Remember, just because these habits have been normalized, does not mean they are your normal.

Reflecting on your own daily life habits and behaviours, ask yourself why do you do the things you do? Is it in alignment still? Do you enjoy it? Take stock of what you do. Some things you may realize you do simply because you've done it every day for the last 10 years. Some habits, or routines are incredible. It doesn't mean you need to disrupt everything, but it is important to occasionally check in and ask yourself, "why do I do the things I do?"

There is no wrong answer for why you do the things you do. There is no shame in doing something because it makes you feel like you belong, or are a part of something bigger than yourself. Part of accepting who you are, and who you want to be, is in acknowledging why you do what you do. Check in with yourself regularly, to make sure what you are doing, the habits that make up your day, and the days which make up your life is aligned. Are you living them for you?

Make your day and your habits work for you now. Not for who you were five, ten or even one year ago. Things change. You change. You evolve, and adapt and that's the beauty of this life. You *get* to change!

Beliefs

Our beliefs are so deeply ingrained in us, when someone questions them, our human instinct is to get defensive. But what if we sat with curiosity and listened to other beliefs? We could try them on for size and decide whether we want to keep our own beliefs. Perhaps we can adapt or even take on new beliefs.

The trouble with being a human, is we often pick a belief or a truth and stick with it, without ever pausing to question or re-evaluate. As we learn and experience more, it should be expected that our truth will grow and adapt. Our ego likes to keep us "safe" in what it knows, and it can feel like a threat if someone questions what you believe to be true.

> "It may be a perfectly good belief,
> but it may not be yours anymore."
>
> Jennie Schimanski

Beliefs show up in all areas of our lives. What do we believe to be true about the world around us? What do we believe to be normal in our lives and in society around us? There are so many things that could fall under this category, but there are three I want to share as examples.

Self-Doubting Beliefs

These are the beliefs we were perhaps told when we were little. For example, as a child you were told you were not smart or athletic. If you were told this enough times, or if the moment you were told this was surrounded by big emotions, we can subconsciously choose to believe it.

If you were told over and over that you were not smart, and you didn't do well in school, those lower marks on your report card would start to cement the idea within you that you are not smart. When this happens, we start to act like we are not smart. Our mind is so powerful, we will continue to prove ourself right by getting poor grades. We can self-sabotage our grades in order to fully make those beliefs true. As an example, if you knew you had a test coming up and believed that you were not smart, the story you might have told yourself could have looked like: 'there's no point in me studying, I'm not going to pass anyways.' And if you didn't study, chances are your marks would reflect that, further proving to yourself that you are not smart.

Another way to look at this common belief, is that perhaps you are smart, but you don't learn well in the way the school system teaches. If you were a kid who needed to understand how things worked, often memorizing facts for tests wouldn't make sense for you. It is not that you are not smart, it is the system that doesn't work for you. What beliefs do you have about yourself that are in fact old or mislead stories that are no longer serving you? Can you start to look, now as an adult, at what else may have made you believe them to be true? And ask yourself, is this still true?

With any of your beliefs try to remember the first moment you remember that belief being a part of you. For instance, if you were not athletic, where did this idea stem from? As an example, maybe you were really good at some sports, but you were not very good at baseball. If you were up to bat during a practice or gym class and constantly missed the ball, you would start to doubt your abilities. If another kid or adult teased you, or pointed out your lack of skill in front of everyone, chances are you were really embarrassed. When we don't acknowledge how we feel in the moment, we tend to associate that feeling with the circumstance. And to avoid feeling that way again, we avoid that circumstance. So, if you were made fun of for having an off day, or for lacking a particular skill, it can quickly spiral into a generalization like 'I am not athletic'. It's safer as far as your ego is concerned to avoid all chances where you may experience that feeling again, rather than to try it another time or with a different sport. What do you avoid doing because of an old belief? Does that belief have any truth to it, or have you made it far bigger than it needs to be?

Business Beliefs

In business, and in the hustle mindset of the personal development world, realizing that it was okay to change my mind and question the systems, was a huge lesson.

Numbers are used to compare, and rank where you stand amongst your competitors. However, I've learned over the years, that a lot of people show these big, flashy numbers of success. What they sometimes hide is the expenses, the burn out and the stress that goes on behind the scenes. It's one thing to be successful on paper, and on social media. However, if it's not balanced with a healthy, fulfilling lifestyle, it's going to crash one day. Or you are going to crash one day.

The hustle culture has been popular for years, and I think it is slowly (thankfully) finding a better balance. Sometimes, we need to hustle and work hard, but when it's the only side of the business world that you are operating in, it can be detrimental. We have been taught that in order to be successful, you must work hard – this is a belief I'd encourage you to question.

What we are starting to see shift, is that you can hustle with heart from a heart led business. Inspiring leaders find the hustle and the heart and drive their business from impact, knowing the sales will follow.

What I have started to believe is that when things get hard, it's often something bigger than us trying to teach us a lesson to grow to the next phase of who we are here to be. When things continue to be hard, it's often a sign that we are on the wrong path. Life gets to be easy. It gets to be effortless, the majority of the time. It's all about finding that balance of hustle and flow. Allow yourself to look at alternative options or beliefs when something starts to feel off. Trust that your intuition is guiding you to see things differently.

Religious Beliefs

Did you grow up believing in religion, in God, in the Universe? For myself, I grew up going to the United Church. When I was a kid, we had a fantastic and entertaining minister. The attendance was full, the Sunday school was fun, and I loved getting dressed up each Sunday to go. As I got older, less and less families started going, and I started to resent having to go to church every week. It wasn't fun anymore, and especially when I was too old for Sunday school.

For a few years, I felt like I didn't resonate with what the church stood for. I didn't understand why I had to physically go to the building to talk about God. It just didn't make sense to me. Yet it was something my family had always done, and so we went. It was rarely questioned, if ever.

I got to the point when I was 16 that I decided I must be an Atheist. But using that title didn't feel right either. I lived in a fog of not knowing what I believed for many years. Leaning into Spiritual Development, I now believe in the Universe and in Spirit and Source. I also believe there can be God and the Universe simultaneously. For example, if *my* truth is currently a belief in the Universe, *your* truth can be in God. And we can co-exist in this world together, happily ever after. *My* truth may also change as I grow and learn more about myself. Just because it is my truth now, does not mean it will be my truth forever. The same goes for you – you get to decide. You get to re-evaluate and determine what your current beliefs are. And they are allowed to change.

What other beliefs do you have about how you should act, behave or be in this world? Do they still resonate with you, or is it time to re-evaluate them? This is part of the journey of unlearning who we once were or thought we had to be, in order to accept and become the maven that we are. That's the beauty of this life – it gets be filled with continual learnings and unlearnings.

Seasons

"We do not see the world as it is,
but the world is as we see it."

Unknown

Throughout our life, we go through many seasons - just like in nature. If we think about this like the four seasons, it might look something like this:

- Winter is when we go within and often want to retreat. We want time alone and time for reflection.
- Spring shows up when new ideas are ready, when we're ready to start a new project, or explore a new idea or hobby. We spring into action!
- Summer is often when we have the most energy and desire a full social calendar and have lots on the go.
- Autumn is when we let go of what is no longer serving us, we re-evaluate what we want to continue working on or who we want to spend time with in the next season.

An Extra Dose of Magic

Just like nature, women's menstrual cycles have seasons too. We have a season of winter and hibernation mode (during our bleed), a season of spring where things are being planted and rejuvenated, a season of summer (during our ovulation) when our bodies are ready to have an egg fertilized and grow into a baby and our season of autumn, when our bodies are getting ready to shed their lining. This is also reflected in the energy you will have around your period cycle. I highly recommend tracking your cycle, and start to notice when you need quiet days of rest for yourself (winter), and when you are energized to create or have a full social calendar (summer).

There are a lot of fantastic resources out there, here I have put it in the simplest of terms. If this interests you, please explore other mavens that have created wonderful pieces of work about this.

Within these seasons, we will also experience another layer of them; such as seasons of triumph and glory, and seasons of sadness and heartache. In the midst of these seasons, it can be hard to remember that they are in fact seasons. They are temporary and they are leading us smoothly into the next phase of our lives.

Throughout our whole life, we are going through seasons; of growth, of learning, and of discovery. Like seasons in nature, it's okay when they come to an end. If fact, one season must end for a new season to flourish.

When we are avoiding our next season or step, resistance can show up in the form of self-sabotage. Things such as imposter syndrome, fear of success, fear of being seen or fear of failure. We will self-sabotage in order to halt the process, for example, by avoiding making the phone call or appointment we need to make. We will procrastinate on what we know will take us to the next level.

Imposter Syndrome is the feeling of 'who am I to do that?' or 'who do I think I am?' This often comes up when we are stepping into a new path and we think, 'I don't have the qualifications, or the education to do that'. Fear of success and fear of being seen often go hand in hand. It can be the narrative that success brings visibility, and visibility brings unwanted attention. Fear of Failure often stops us in our tracks in a mindset of why would I even try, I'm going to fail anyways, so I might as well not even do the thing I want to try.

All of these can show up in various ways. They often have deep rooted points of origin, stemming from childhood or even from past lives. If you notice these are your patterns, start to ask yourself why? Sit with why you fear that, or why you self-sabotage? Initially, you may not notice, but the more you reflect and venture into personal development, the more visible the patterns become. Once you have an awareness of your patterns, you can start to look more closely at where they originate from. In order to heal, the first step is in becoming aware of what you desire to be healed.

For now, simply start to notice what season you are in, or have been in recently. Notice how long you've been in this season; does it feel like it's just beginning or are you starting to feel restless or excited to move into the next? If you are feeling "stuck" in a season, ask yourself, 'what lesson do I still need to learn here?'

Here are a few of the most common seasons I have witnessed with clients, and throughout my own journey.

Seasons Of Identity

We create identities for ourselves in the titles that we hold or the characteristics that we embrace. It's easy to slip into a place where we don't know who we are, outside of these identities.

As a child, I loved drawing, and painting, and I excelled at art. I was constantly painting my room, and re-arranging furniture. I was drawing blueprints for my dream house complete with a library resembling ones in fairytales, and secret passageways from room to room throughout. That carried out into my adult life as I studied and practiced interior design. After about ten years, I was restless and knew I was meant to be shifting my focus and spending more time with personal development and organizing events. Deciding to stop being a designer took years as I had identified as a designer for so long. There were a lot of yeses that maybe should have been nos and resistance to change as I started to shift away from being an 'Interior Designer'.

I have had many seasons of identity throughout my life so far: babysitter, big sister, lifeguard, florist, waitress, receptionist, car and bus detailer, designer, tutor, college professor, library assistant, and entrepreneur. For myself, this is ever-evolving as I learn new skills and as my curiosity peaks in different areas of interest. I have had a lot of judgement towards myself over the years as I tried to fit into the boxes of society. Mostly because we are taught to choose just one – but who really knows from such a young age what they want to do with their life? It's okay if you want to try a different title on for size, to see how it feels.

> "...those who do not attempt to appear more than they are but are simply themselves, stand out as remarkable and are the only ones who truly make a difference in the world."

> Eckhart Tolle, A New Earth

When I was finally starting to realize I was ready to no longer be only a designer, I had to ask myself, who am I? What do I love about who I am? When doing this yourself, try removing the "job title" from your description. And remove the role you play in your family home. Being a mother or father, a wife or husband, a daughter or son, and a sister or brother; these are honourable titles. And I do not want to discredit them at all. I do want to remind you, that there is so much value in who you are beyond those titles. Who were you before you were a mother? Who were you when it was just you? When your soul was all you had to ask?

Ask yourself, who have I forgotten that I am? Often these roles we play, either professionally or personally, take over. We start to mold ourselves to fit into someone else's expectations of what we should be or how we should act. Compromise is okay, as long as you are staying true to who you are and what your soul needs. In any role, if you compromise your essence, your energy will be depleted, and you will no longer represent your true self. This is debilitating for both you and the people who expect you to remain who you were when you first took on the role that they see you in. By you reclaiming who you are, you will show up vibrationally higher. This is the version of you they should want to know if they are the right people for you.

Journal Prompts Seasons of Identity:
1. Who am I?
2. What do I love about who I am?
3. Who were you when it was just you?
4. Who do you desire to be?
5. How do you desire to feel?
6. Who have I forgotten who I am?

Looking back on this, I will always be a designer. I am designing a life I love. But I am not defined by being a designer. I am so much more. I am an artist. I have a gypsy soul and an undeniable need for adventure and travel. I am also a daughter, a sister, a friend.

But first and foremost, I am a soul living in a human body. I am here to experience all that life has to offer, regardless of how it defines me. I am (insert your name here).

That's it. That's all I need to know about you. Because who you are is not defined by a title. Who you are shows up in how you treat other people, in how you light up when you talk about the things you love. When you are beaming with pride over your accomplishments and when you can feel the love pour out of you for the life you are leading.

This reflection of who you really are can be uncomfortable, especially if you've become removed over the years from who you are on a soul level. You have the ability to find yourself again. To return to yourself, or to create a new version. This is your permission to set out on this journey of changing seasons. This is your permission to show up as the maven that you are. To evolve into your next version of yourself. Knowing this doesn't change you, it only adds to your awareness of self. It's a deeper understanding of who you are and of who you are becoming.

It is also okay to grieve the old versions of you. As you move into a new season, there sometimes is a polarity between being excited for what's to come, and the sense of loss of what is no longer. I see this a lot in new moms. They are thrilled to be new moms and excited for this chapter to begin. And there's an underlying sadness we don't always allow moms to grieve, or they don't think they can, because they are so excited for this stage of their life. There is a version of your single life that will never be again. Perhaps there were things you loved doing on your own, or things you thought you'd do before you became a mom that you're now realizing aren't a priority anymore. Even though you maybe don't really want those pieces of your life anymore, you can still grieve the version of you that once did. Both can be true. This happens in other areas of our life too, where we grieve past versions of ourselves or versions of ourselves that didn't get to fully come to fruition.

Who you were served a purpose, and that version of you deserves to be remembered. That version is still within you, and aspects of that part of you can be called on at any time, even if that season is over. It just may look a little different than it used to, and that's okay. That's part of the beauty of your identity, it gets to evolve as you do!

Seasons Of Growth

All of the seasons we go through have the power to teach us and the ability to let us grow. If we choose to ignore these lessons, you will be given these lessons, over and over and over again. You are here, in this lifetime to grow and to expand. There are lessons you need to learn in order to move onto the next stage of your journey, so if you choose to ignore these lessons, the Universe, will keep delivering them to you, until you see it for what it really is. Pay attention.

Seasons of growth are when we are craving to learn and expand our knowledge, when we are trying to soak up as much as we can. When I first started my own business as an Interior Designer, I was craving connection as an entrepreneur. I went to every conference I could in that season. A conference on Wealth and Money in Toronto, which led me to a conference in Calgary all about Joint Ventures and Business Masterminds. I had joined a Network Marketing company and was attending the Canadian and International events. I was searching for community and in that seeking knowledge, opening doors until I found the right one. That season of growth led me to recognizing the value of events, and community. It allowed me to recognize that most people in this world are also looking for community, and it greatly inspired the beginning of my business, The Maven Project.

Although, I have continued attending conferences and events over the years, there also comes a point in each season where you need to take a different action. I started to feel called to create an event, instead of simply attend. These feelings of 'okay, I've absorbed as much as I can right now, I'm going to burst if I don't do something with it'. That's when you know a season is shifting. It doesn't need to be big, or bold, but instead of watching all of the YouTube videos about how to paint, eventually it becomes time to pick up a paint brush and try it. There is so much growth in that stage as well.

Tara Westover shares in her book *Educated*, "first, find out what you're capable of, then decide who you are". So often we create this idea of who we should be, without really knowing ourselves. The more we educate ourselves with new ideas, new people and new surroundings the more we learn about how capable we truly are. The seasons of growth are simply adding another piece to the puzzle that is your story. Some pieces take longer to find than others, and some fit in right away.

Seasons of Failure

"You're going to be happy," said life.
"But first I'm going to make you strong."

Unknown

We're given failures and successes because we need to learn from both. Without one the other loses its relevance. It can't all be easy. During these difficult seasons, I embrace the mantra:

I am willing to see this differently.
I choose to see love instead.

A simple re-frame, after the feelings are felt, and it's time to shift out of the sadness that failure brings. How can you start to find the lessons within your failures? What did they teach you? Who did they connect you with? How did you react? Would you do anything differently next time?

I ask that last question, because our failures are often preparing us for what's next. A bigger leap or a better opportunity may be coming. Those failures remind us that we can go through a lot, and our "worst case scenario" after living it, isn't always as bad as we perceived it would be.

"All experience is valid, but learned
experience creates change."

Ruth Montgomery, Journal Entry

Failures can also be viewed as a re-direction. They are a beautiful opportunity to see where it's time to re-direct your energy. If you keep applying for the same type of job and aren't getting any offers, is it perhaps because you are meant to be doing something else? When things keep going wrong, like you got into a minor car accident, or injured yourself, start to take note of where you were going when it happened. Maybe you're not supposed to be going there? Is it a job you've stayed at too long, or a relationship that you know is over? Start to pay attention to your failures, and ask, what am I supposed to learn from this?

It was interesting when I fell and broke my shoulder after falling down a flight of stairs, my mind immediately went to curiosity. What am I supposed to learn from this? Previously, I would have been frustrated and so upset, thinking that I didn't have time for this and what am I going to do?

But this time, as I was laying on the floor waiting for the ambulance, I asked my brother to grab a couple of reference books for me and look up the different significance of what I had injured. I knew that my shoulder was broken, my two front teeth were chipped, and that my leg was bruised but not broken. There were two big lessons that came out of that fall, one being, it was time to finish this book, and two, it's okay to receive support. Lessons, that had both been whispering in my ear that I had been ignoring for the few weeks leading up to this experience.

Journal Prompts Seasons of Failure:
1. What did they teach you?
2. Who did they connect you with?
3. How did you react?
4. Would you do anything differently next time?
5. What am I supposed to learn from this?

In the seasons of failure, I also find it's helpful to release any expectations of where you thought you should be, or need to be. Your journey, is yours, and yours alone. It isn't meant to look like anyone else's – so stop comparing it to an unrealistic expectation.

When it feels like the world is against you or nothing is working, try to find gratitude in the small moments throughout your day. Did you enjoy your coffee today? Perhaps buy yourself a fresh bouquet of flowers, or go for a walk and feel the sunshine on your face. It's the simple things, that bring so much meaning when life feels tough. It will get better, I promise you, it's simply a season. Try to find the lesson in the season, because the sooner you reflect and learn the lesson, the sooner you can move through it.

Seasons Of Triumph

Seasons of triumph and success are easy to see the benefit in. They are exhilarating and can be life-changing. You are riding on such a high during these seasons, that you feel like nothing can stop you. These seasons are amazing! Soak it all in and remember to be present in the moment.

Don't look for what could go wrong.

Don't look to what happens next.

Don't apologize for it.

Just be in that moment. Enjoy it. Celebrate it. Integrate it.

Take a deep breath in and feel that. Let your body fill with the abundance of it all.

You deserve every ounce of love and joy that a season of triumph brings!

One of my favourite seasons of triumph was announcing Camp Maven to the world in 2018. I had had an idea to create Camp Maven, had a brainstorming session with some incredible women, and finally got the push to put an event up on Facebook. It went viral. Within 72 hours of posting the event it was seen by 137,000 people and when tickets were made available for sale shortly after that, Camp Maven sold out with 150 attendees in 12 hours. This was a wild experience. It felt like I had put this idea out in the world to see if there was any interest and the Universe took it and ran, as if to say there's no turning back now! I will forever be grateful to all of the volunteers, camp counsellors, speakers and attendees who joined me on this adventure and made it what it was. I could not have done it without all of the incredible mavens that were there – and I would not have wanted to. The community we all created together was like no other!

It's important to celebrate these seasons – no matter how big or small! When Camp Maven went viral, a soul sister of mine and I popped a bottle of champagne! I keep the cork from that bottle on my bookshelf as a reminder of that moment of triumph and exhilaration! I encourage you to find a way to celebrate yourself, and your seasons of triumph. Maybe it's champagne, or a fancy night out! Perhaps it's buying yourself something to mark the occasion, or treat yourself to an experience you've been wanting to try. Perhaps it's a bubble bath or a walk in the forest. It doesn't matter what it is or how much it costs, the simple and intentional act of taking a moment to celebrate yourself is what matters. This allows your body to stay in that high vibrational energy long enough to integrate this next level.

Seasons Of Sadness

These are the tough seasons. These are the moments when we like to hide from the world and pretend that everything is okay. These are the ones that are hard to talk about as we are going through them. There are so many feelings associated with heartache. Guilt. Shame. Embarrassment. All equally uncomfortable and ridden with sadness.

The worst part of these seasons, is we often feel the need to isolate ourselves, causing us to feel alone. Loneliness in itself, can be a season of heartache.

The following are taken from earlier journal entries of mine throughout the past couple of years: *What is my place in the world? Why am I here if no one understands? What am I meant to be doing? I don't feel like myself. But who is that really? I feel lost, and in a daze. What is wrong with me? Wait, why do I think anything is wrong with me? Where is this coming from?*

Have you ever thought any of these questions? Know that you are not alone in those thoughts. Have you ever told anyone you have had those feelings? Why do we feel we cannot share these with other people?

One of the best things you can do for yourself through your journey, is to learn how to be okay with yourself in the quiet moments. Turn off the television, put down your phone. And just be. Write down what comes into your head, and see where your mind wanders. Who are you without all of the noise? Do you even know what you want? Or have you become so accustomed to tuning your inner voice out and using methods of distraction to avoid hearing what your soul already knows?

We've all had seasons of sadness and heartache. Before I tell you about one of my toughest seasons, I encourage you to write down a few of your own. What comes to mind when you think of heartache? Where have you suffered? Where have you been hurt? Who has hurt you? Why did it hurt? Just make a list. Expand on them if you feel called, or if it's still too painful, simply right down a name or a place. Writing these down helps your body energetically release any stagnant energy you've been holding onto. Let yourself cry, and feel any emotions that come up when you're remembering these moments. This is part of the healing journey – we must feel our emotions in order to release them.

"Hard things make the easy exciting. There needs to be a level of comparison for what's next so you don't question how real it is. In the tough moments, remember, this is just your level of comparison for what's next."

Ruth Montgomery, August 2020 Journal Entry

Grief and depression - the emotions that will suck all of the life out of you, and make you question everything. Even as I write this, I am starting to tear up at the feeling of grief and all the layers that it entails. Parts of this section have been written from the depths of my own grief, so as you are reading my words, if you feel the sudden wave of emotions or urge to cry come over you, let it. Let the depths of your emotions come through to be released. Sometimes the mind doesn't need to be reminded why, it just is.

trigger warning: suicide, depression
I am by no means an expert in this, this section is completely from my own lived experience, and if you are experiencing grief or depression, please seek guidance. You do not have to go through this alone. You are not alone, even when it feels, at its depth, that no one understands. Please seek the support you need and desire.

My journey into this realm of personal development, also partially began as I was seeking answers over the loss of a loved one. A family member I loved very much, and couldn't understand the emotions I was going through at the time.

The first stages of grief, for me, were pain and guilt. Guilty that I didn't do more, and pain over the loss I was experiencing. And very quickly for me, anger set in. I was so mad. Livid at how it had all played out.

"I was wrecked. I was so angry at him. How could he do that? Why did he think that that was his only option? Why didn't he seek more help? Why didn't I do more? Why didn't I take him seriously? Why? Why didn't I see it coming? Why didn't I understand the severity of what was happening? Why didn't I tell him how much I loved him? Why did he have to leave me?

I yelled and I screamed at him. To him. For him. I cried for days on end. It was a grief I had never experienced and would never wish on anyone. How could he leave us like that and not think that we cared? How could he not understand how much it would hurt those he left behind? How could he not see how missed he would be?"

These stages happened quickly for me, and where I got stuck was in the depression, reflection and loneliness stage.

I have done a lot of inner work on this and I share this because if you have gone through something similar, you are not alone. I have struggled with the impact that this moment has had on my life, because ultimately, his story is not mine to tell. But my grief is mine. What I experienced following this is mine. It will be different than everyone else whose life he touched, so I cannot comment on their experience, or even begin to know what yours may have been if you've lost a loved one.

Over the years following this heartache, I have experienced feelings of depression. From moments of, "My spark, my ambition is gone. I feel numb. I am going through a period of depression. I don't even want to use the energy to write this. Wtf. I am tired. It's not even 9am."

I think, from personal experience, a lot of times a death of a loved one, or loss of something, allows us the space where grief is okay, and those lower emotions are accepted by others for a time. It can be a gateway into some of the other lower emotions that we've been suppressing.

It's like, the emotions see the opportunity to come out, to be released, to be exposed and explored and you don't know what hits you. It's all of a sudden too much and not enough at the same time.

I imagine it, like many things in life, like a pendulum. We get stuck swinging so far to one side, that when something shifts, we dramatically go as far as we possibly can to the other side. Because we've spent so much time on one side of the pendulum, it's like we feel we have to make up for lost time. When really all we want to do is find the balance in the middle. The sweet spot where both make sense.

"I have been so emotional lately. I have never felt a depression like I have this week. Thoughts of how easy it would be to disappear and make all of my problems go away. I know I am meant for greater things so I would never, but this is my current state."

Ruth Montgomery, December 2018 Journal Entry

This came during a three-week period at the lowest, I have ever experienced. More than four and a half years after the passing of a loved one, yet leading up to the fifth anniversary of that particular experience. Now, this isn't to say it's related, but our emotions are all so intertwined, and what came out of this experience for me was related.

I remember laying in the bathtub one night, living on my own, where the thought passed through: "This is it. I get it. I get how easy it would be to disappear. To just not wake up tomorrow."

In that moment, I had an out-of-body experience. All of a sudden, I was above myself looking down thinking, "who the fuck do you think you are? How dare you make a decision like this or even contemplate this if you are not willing to give the people who would be hurt by this the most a chance to save you?"

Two things happened from that experience, that cemented my belief in something greater than us, call it God, Source, Spirit, The Universe, whatever your heart desires or resonates with, but I believe there is something out there connecting us all.

First, my dad messaged me a short while later. Normally my mum is in tune with my energy, and has that mother's intuition that something is wrong, so because it was my dad, and he took the time to message, just made it that much clearer. He messaged out of nowhere, saying "Are you okay?" He had no reason, on a human consciousness level to think I wasn't okay. I responded saying, "Actually I'm not. How did you know?" He said he didn't know, he just had a feeling that he needed to message, and immediately offered whatever support I needed. Did I need to come stay with them, did I need him to come see me, did I need to talk, and so on.

There are a couple of points I want to make with this. One – if you ever, and I mean EVER, have a feeling that you need to message someone, because something feels off, and you can't explain it. Please do. You have no idea what impact your message or phone call may make. Move all of your human emotions of fear or looking "crazy" out of the way and trust that there is a reason you are feeling that urge. And if you're wrong? So what? But if you're right, you maybe just reminded that person that they are not alone when they needed it most.

Two – There is a difference between offering sympathy and understanding from empathy. I realized from this that I had been talking for years from a deep understanding of grieving a victim of suicide. Yet I did not have the first-hand experience to empathize with someone experiencing the thoughts of suicide. And this is not something, I wish on anyone, yet this deeper awareness of just how real it was brought so much clarity to the work I was doing.

Sometimes, we have to experience something, so that we can relate and better understand from a first-person experience what someone else is going through to help in their healing process.

2018 Reflection on my Depression
"I don't think I could ever commit suicide. I was low enough to understand how easy it would be for someone to commit suicide though. The isolation, loneliness, sorry for myself, life not going my way, no clue what next step would be – that I got. And the worst part was that I didn't want to "bother" anyone with those thoughts. I didn't want to bring down or hinder their bliss in the moment.

But who am I to even contemplate suicide if I'm not willing to give my family or closest friends the chance to save me. The ones that would be left on Earth to be hurt. I am also not the version of myself I want people to remember. I'm selfish and isolating myself because I don't like who I am in this season. That's not me. I'm ready to embrace who I am. But I had to explore these depths to be able to relate to others. To be able to have empathy to their story. To be able to connect on a deeper level. I know what it feels like to be that low. I can now relate personally to some degree, as the person going through suicidal thoughts, the person grieving suicide and all that that involves leading up to it and after. It's part of my journey."

I had to explore these depths to not only provide sympathy for the person grieving, but to have the personal understanding to be able to show up with empathy for the person experiencing these emotions. These emotions are part of my journey in helping others awaken to see their potential. To see their value here – on this Earth.

Through all of our seasons, we have to accept ourselves fully, flaws and all, to encourage others to accept themselves fully. This was just one of my seasons. And I may find myself here again, but I know I will find myself on the other side again too – stronger and with a deeper understanding of self.

Secondly, this experience brought a lot of understanding for me, and an awareness about how mental health is perceived in our world. We are going through a period of time where people are starting to awaken to their higher consciousness and awareness to self. The weight of the world is heavy, and the souls that are here to help raise the vibration of the planet are feeling that weight even more so. These people are tuning into their souls. To their inner voice. Yet typically, when we express that we are hearing voices, we are labelled as "crazy". You are not crazy. You are awake, and aware of your inner voice. That voice is your soul calling you to listen. To wake up and become the maven that you are. Step into your power.

A message for the grieving soul, for the soul at a depth
so low suicide has crossed your mind.
This is not your time. You are not going crazy.
You are not alone and **we need you here**.
We need you here, physically on planet
earth as the beautiful human being that you are.
We have work to do. You have work to do
(when you're ready). Welcome to the journey!

A Few Other Seasons of Importance:

Seasons of Selfishness & Seasons of Service
There are some seasons meant to be of service and some that are just meant for you. It's okay to step back and be completely selfish sometimes and take care of yourself.

If some part of your soul is calling you to do more or be more, or part of you feels like you're missing a piece of the puzzle, know that there can be more to life than what you've got. There can also be less. Have you added too much to your life to try to be everything to everyone? Is your life overflowing yet feels empty? Have you lost touch with who you are at your core?

A reminder from my Spirit Guides: "Just take care of you. Stop trying to help others – just be the example."

Seasons of Creation & Seasons of Consumption

In personal and spiritual development, it's easy to get sucked into always desiring more. More information, more courses, and more programs. We are being sold to constantly. There are so many experts that are priceless, and there is so much you can learn from the people who have gone before you in this work. At some point though, we have to stop and absorb all of the information and the lessons. We have to give our soul time to embody and integrate it all.

Think about your stomach when you're eating. You can eat and eat and eat, but at some point, your belly gets full. If you keep eating beyond that, you will puke. Your body will physically reject the food you are trying to give it. Your stomach needs time to digest the food, process it, and expel the parts that it doesn't need, keeping the nutrients that add value.

This is what happens with bringing in new information as well. At a certain point there's no more room to learn more. Your body needs time to process and reflect on what it has learned. To embody and absorb the information and tools that serve you. And to expel the pieces that don't make sense to you.

Taking on new information or courses is productive and beneficial until you hit the point of being full. After that, when you keep consuming, constant "learning" can become a crutch from actually integrating and growing. It looks good to outsiders, it feels good to the ego, but it hinders your growth. It can become a form of self-sabotage, limiting you from moving to your next level. It makes you feel overwhelmed and sick. Our bodies can only handle so much consumption. At this point, taking a pause to digest everything, and to possibly create something with all that you've learned.

This could be anything from that new business idea you've been preparing for, to taking time to bring out your inner artist and play. Creating with your hands (such as art or gardening), creating and moving with your body (such as music or dance), or creating with your soul (such as meditation or writing).

An Extra Dose of Magic: Numbing versus Nourishing

There is a time and a place for numbing out, yet there is a difference between numbing out to forget or avoid, and to nourish for rest and rejuvenation.

When was the last time you sat in silence, with only your thoughts? We often get into a cycle of always having something on to distract us, whether it's the television, the radio, a podcast, music, or a book we are reading. All of which can be amazing, and much needed. Where I want to bring your attention to is are you relaxing and resting during this, or are you avoiding something?

You know the nights you sit down to watch a movie and you sink right into it? Oblivious of anything that you "should" be doing, and you're able to fully relax and enjoy it.

What about the nights when you sit down, and watch a movie and the whole time, you're scrolling on your phone, or thinking about what you "should" or "could" be doing instead? Feeling worse as the time passes for "wasting time".

That's the difference between nourishing and numbing. Distractions have their time and place, absolutely. What I encourage you to do is to start to be aware as it's happening. Instead of waiting for the movie to be over and feeling panicked about what you should have done, check in with yourself during, and start to ask yourself as it's happening. If you notice then, that it feels like you're avoiding something, turn the movie off and go do whatever would be more beneficial for yourself.

The more we start to practice this awareness, the easier it gets to trust our intuition and to know that we do, in fact, know what we need to do, to live the life we desire.

Numbing can show up on our spiritual awakening as we're getting to a new level, when our ego is in resistance of what's next. I refer to this as journeying through the fog – the stage where you've released some of your old beliefs, connections or ventures, but can't see what's next. It feels like we're in a pause or a plateau, and our ego doesn't know what to do. Our ego will resort to old habits, perhaps self-sabotaging ones to keep us small. Like eating comfort food, that we know isn't fueling our best selves, or drinking alcohol to "forget" thinking about what we're doing with our lives. For me, I know I'm avoiding a lesson, or clarity for the next level when I'm avoiding journaling.

Seasons of Rest & Seasons of Transition

When I was traveling solo in November of 2021, I had a moment in Italy where I felt like I needed to leave; it was time to move to a new country, and I needed to make decisions quickly. On my way out of Italy I stopped to see the Leaning Tower of Pisa and was reminded just how important support is in moments like that. The construction on the tower began in 1173 and as per the information plaque, "It was designed to stand 185 feet (56 metres) high and was constructed of white marble. Three of its eight stories had been completed when the uneven settling of the building's foundations in the soft ground became noticeable. At that time, war broke out between the Italian city-states, and construction was halted for almost a century. This pause allowed the tower's foundation to settle and likely prevented its early collapse." Over the years, experts have been called in to support, and re-structure the building foundation, the ground beneath her and even adjust the materials being used to continue building her to what we see now!

This tower can teach us that if she had not of paused, to re-evaluate her path she would have most definitely collapsed. And in that pause, she had a team of support help in her re-building. Had it not been for her team, she would not still be standing today. And expecting to stand for at least another 200 years.

The season of rest, in between seasons, especially after a season of growth is important to integrate what you've learned. To take the time to rest, reflect and re-connect to where you want to be. Chances are you've learned something in that season that will alter the direction you were headed. If you push through and keep going down the "wrong" direction, eventually you'll get so far off course that it will take even longer to re-direct.

I do not think there are wrong directions exactly, for each season and path has lessons available to us. I do believe though, the longer we are off course so to speak, the longer it takes to get back to a place of fulfillment and ease.

Sometimes, the seasons transition from one to the next with a bit of overlap. The season I am currently in for instance, of writing this book. This has been a season for the last two years, although it has come and gone in and amongst other seasons and life lessons. The last few months or so, professionally and spiritually, it has felt as though I need to finish this book in order for the next season to start to arrive. The feeling that finishing this book, will be the piece that unlocks the next season, and that I'm not meant to know what this is until I have that final bit.

Other times things can drop in quite abruptly. For instance, when I learned Reiki, I felt sure that it was the piece I was missing. And before I even finished my training, I knew it was simply another incredible tool to add to my puzzle.

The last few months, have felt like I've been looking down a very long tunnel as I'm healing from my shoulder injury. As my shoulder is gaining mobility, and this book is reaching completion, I have this overwhelming feeling of seeing the light at the end of the tunnel. And although I cannot see beyond the end of the tunnel, I know with all of my being that I am going to burst through into this brilliant, brightly lit world. Through the tunnel there is a world I'm not even aware of. Like many seasons, this is part of the unfolding. It is part of the magic that is our journey. I don't know what's next, and I don't need to. I get to trust that it will all work out for my greatest and highest good. I get to trust that the opportunities and the people that are meant to be in my life will find me, and as long as I keep following the nudges, I will be guided exactly where I am supposed to be – whatever that looks like! The same goes for you! Trust in the process.

As you are moving forward, remember to look back and acknowledge how far you've come and celebrate all that you have accomplished.

A Thought on Goal Setting

Life isn't going to take you where you think it should. The path is never going to be as easy or as smooth as you think it could be. And really, what's the fun in that?

Have you ever gone for a walk – from point A to B? Straight down the street on a mission? So focused on where you are going that you miss what's happening around you?

What about a casual walk – on a trail? Still aiming for Point B but with no real timeline to get there. Do you stop to look around? Do you stop to explore or investigate what's growing around you? If you pass someone, do you stop to talk? Or at least smile and say hello as they pass you?

It's the same in life, when we are in a rush to get to the goal, we miss the juicy stuff. The stuff life is made out of. The experiences that shape who we are, and impact our lives. Those are the moments that make the destination worthwhile.

If you are so quick to get to the end – you get there and find you're there before everyone else, sitting, waiting, anxious for everyone else to arrive for the meeting to get started. Watching as the others stroll in, relaxed, happy and laughing about their journey – simply so carefree with not a worry on their mind.

That's what life is all about. The experiences, the people you meet, and the joy you gain from that. Our paths often aren't straightforward. It's in the pauses and side trails that we gain more clarity or the tools we actually need to keep going. In personal development, we often hear about goal setting. The narrative is often to set a goal and work towards that goal doing whatever it takes. The beauty of "hustle" culture. I fully believe in the power of goal setting because we need to have something to work towards to keep pushing us forward. However, the initial "goal" is often not where we're supposed to end up. In the journey to the goal, we open ourselves up to new opportunities and connections. It is often one of those new pieces that we would have never found had we not been working our way towards the initial goal. That little detour, is often the true goal we didn't know we desired.

You must be open to exploring your curiosity if you want to continue to grow, and trust that it's guiding you to exactly where you are meant to be. Especially in the moments when it seems irrelevant to the goal. Approach it with curiosity and wonder, let it guide you in its own magic.

My sister and I were walking the beach one day last summer looking for sea glass. Generally, we will find 1-3 pieces of sea glass on a walk, in greens, whites and the odd blue piece. This day, I was looking specifically for a rare piece of purple sea glass. We walked further than we normally would, and unfortunately, we didn't find any purple. We did however find an abundance of green, white, blue and brown. 20 pieces to be exact. Had we not been determined to find a piece of purple we would have missed three quarters of what we found. It was a beautiful reminder from Mother Nature that abundance is everywhere. Opportunities are everywhere – *if*, you're open to them.

"Often the best opportunities are found on route to other goals that weren't actually meant for you."

Ruth Montgomery, June 2021 Journal Entry

With goal setting, I think it's also important to remember how far we've come when we're looking to set goals for the future. It's so easy to accomplish one thing, and as you're completing it, you're already starting the next. If you travel, think about your last trip. Were you already planning your next vacation while still on your first? It's so easy to get lost in always looking forward that we forget to be in the now. To be present and experiencing the moment.

Wherever you are right now, take a moment to take a deep breath in and acknowledge your surroundings. Where are you? How are you feeling? What is your body trying to tell you? What is one thing near you that brings you joy? What is something you're proud of today?

Before setting new goals, take time to reflect on the lessons you've learned over your life, the past year, and even the past week. Reflecting on past accomplishments, allows us to celebrate ourselves, and to create space mentally and physically for all of the amazing things we have yet to receive. Set a variety of goals:

simple goals that you know you can easily achieve and HUGE, crazy goals that seem so far out of reach. And then be open to opportunities that present themselves along the way.

I love to create a reverse "bucket list" of all of the amazing things I've already accomplished, in my life time and a general reflection on the last year. I do this every year to re-cap and reflect on all of the incredible things I've experienced, accomplished and enjoyed. I also include a list of lessons learned each year of the not so fun experiences, reflecting on what those seasons taught me.

You may never make it to your huge, crazy goal, but I can guarantee you that the goal you end up accomplishing will be far greater than you could have ever imagined. It's the journey when you are aiming towards those goals that will have you gaining more.

Lessons From The Universe

The seasons don't always make sense while we are experiencing them. Especially in the not so fun seasons. The lessons come in the period of reflection after the season.

In the more exciting seasons, we will often be tested along the way. It's as if The Universe is saying, are you sure you really want this? Are you sure you're ready for this next level?

Two years ago, I was selling my house (and the majority of my belongings) and planning on using money from the sale of my furniture to travel for three months. We were days away from accepting offers, with no offers, yet.

"Last night I was saying to my sister 'if it's meant to sell, it will sell, if not that's OK.' She said don't you always say you'll be tested right before the next level? Isn't this a test? If you've still got the beautiful house, are you still going to take the leap? Yes. Yes, I am. I will still travel. I will figure

out how and when. It will happen as it supposed to.
But I have to take the first step."

Ruth Montgomery, August 2021 Journal Entry

Committing to that decision of "I will travel", instead of "I will travel *if* the house sells" set my intention clearly. And we had two offers to accept the next day. It can happen as quickly as that.

It often feels worse before it gets better. The feeling of a contraction in relation to the expansion that is coming. This is mirrored to us in nature constantly, so why would we assume our paths would be any different. Mother Nature is a powerful force that creates forest fires to clear trees so fresh growth can occur. In fact, she prefers to create order out of chaos. It forces us to re-grow, to remind us of the basics, of what matters most to us.

I love the visual of a bow and arrow as well. In order for the arrow to shoot forward with any strength, it must be pulled back, creating resistance with the bow. When we're transitioning through seasons of lessons and growth, there is often that final pull before we are launched fully into the next. Ready to soar!

Ever-Evolving Curiosity

"You can see it for what it is, or you can
imagine what it could be."

Derek Delgaudio's In And Of Itself

We have so many moments in a day and we waste so many on insignificant things. We spend it out of alignment. We spend so much time with the same people, in the same places, filling our time, waiting for the next day, for something better. Those moments that lie in wait add up to a mediocre life and suddenly, days, months, years have gone by and we're still waiting for the better to arrive. Waiting for change to occur.

The people I admire most, create the change. They don't simply wait. They act. Day by day. They create their better. They don't wait idly for someone else to come along and create it for them. They create it. By surrounding themselves with people they love, with places that inspire them and experiences that excite them. By following their curiosities and day by day it gets better.

The beauty of all of this, is that you get to decide what "better" means to you. Your version of better, is yours alone. Follow your curiosities, and let them guide you as you explore this life and this journey of becoming a maven.

"I don't know what the future holds, all I know is that
if I continue to show up authentically – I will
continue to follow my truth."

Ruth Montgomery

An Extra Dose of Magic
You know what you need and what you desire. Through your spiritual awakening or self-development journey you will start to trust yourself more and more. Especially when it comes to diving into your needs, and your emotions. Trust what comes up. Trust that you know. You are the only one that truly knows. You are the maven in your own life. You are a maven. Especially when it comes to you.

PROLOGUE

MAVEN WITHIN

Self-Improvement is really a growing into or of oneself.
You don't need to improve.
You are whole as you are now.
However,
there is always a knowing of self that is going to get deeper.
A self-growth as you become aware.
Nothing *needs* to change,
but it naturally will
as you evolve into knowing yourself better.
Like any relationship deepens and expands.
The one with yourself is the hardest to understand,
but the most important relationship you will ever have.

Ruth Montgomery, Journal Entry from April 2020

We each carry magic within us. Sometimes unknown and hidden to us as adults. But it's there. It lies in your heart.

Your heart knows what you need to do to remind yourself of the magic you have.

Your Inner Child knows what makes it come alive.

Your Higher Self knows what teachers will guide you to unlock the wisdom within you.

They know where to find the key to unlock, to cherish and to embrace your unique magic – the magic that makes you a maven.

What you have to offer the world is unique; your voice and your story are important. No one, not a single other being, will ever have the exact same experiences that you have or will learn what you learn. Ever. You are completely one of a kind. And *you* are a maven.

The truth is, you have always been a maven. You were born a maven. Yet, as we grow up, we are taught to conform and to fit in. To blend into the crowd, to follow a societal checklist just like everyone else. We are taught to rely on experts outside of ourselves for the answers and to strive for someone else's version of success. Somewhere along the way we get lost; distracted from ourselves, and separated from our dreams and desires.

"You are light. You are magic.
It doesn't get any clearer than that."

Ruth Montgomery, March 2019

The journey of Becoming a Maven is a journey of remembering and returning to who you truly are. Of reflecting inward to get to know yourself and to become self-aware. To create self-sovereignty and to find the freedom to be yourself.

A maven, by definition from the Merriam-Webster dictionary, is "one who is experienced or knowledgeable", also known as: an expert. Maven is derived from the Yiddish word, "meyvn" which means "one who understands". Who understands your life more than you? *You* are the maven of your life. You *are* a maven.

A maven is also described as an expert who seeks to pass knowledge onto others. We are all experts at something, we all have a knowledge base that is unique to our life and experiences. This is a term, I believe, in which we all deserve to use and define ourselves as.

It is not defined, necessarily, by our job title or our education. It goes beyond that. It goes into each moment of your life; the ups, the downs, and every experience that you have had. Every conversation that has made you pause, every emotion you've felt and every interaction you've observed.

Becoming a Maven is about taking all of those moments of your life that have brought you here, to this book. It's about being able to step back and understand that without those moments you would not be who you are today. Each piece has shaped or shifted you into the maven that you are.

And for that, I am forever grateful.

Being a maven means standing in your power and in your story. *And* embracing every aspect of it. Taking all of the little pieces and putting it together to be your true self. All of it. Showing up as you, honest, vulnerable and whole. And sharing that knowledge with others, if you so choose.

As mavens, I hope to inspire you to embrace all aspects of yourself. To inspire you to share from a place of vulnerability – because when we share from a place of vulnerability, we give others permission to share as well.

It's also important to remember that your story is always evolving. You are always evolving.

You are allowed to change, grow and adapt, owning your chaos, all while standing in your power as a maven. I welcome you to recognize all that you are and know that, right now, in this moment, you are in the perfect place of your journey.

You are exactly where you are meant to be.

Notice the page numbers on this section.

This is actually the prologue to Becoming a Maven. I have placed it at the end on purpose. To remind you that you have had everything you needed within you this entire time.

You have always been a maven.

This book is here to help you remember these teachings, and to offer a level of understanding that we sometimes are too close to see.

This was inspired by the book *Mary Magdalene Revealed* written by Meggan Watterson. Meggan shares that "Mary Magdalene's gospel starts with missing pages...There was something so incendiary in these first six pages that her gospel starts on page seven."

Now, I am not comparing this book to Mary Magdalene's gospel, but I loved the idea that this information is so important someone in history did not want us to know what those first six pages shared.

Much like how we've always been a maven, and throughout our lives, we forget that vital information. We are taught to forget that.

This is a reclaiming of who you have always been *and* of who you are becoming.

So welcome to this book and to this evolution of becoming a maven.

Thank you for being here, for being a part of this community, and for seeing yourself as the worthy maven that you are.

It's time to awaken the maven within.

To remember and embrace the maven that you are.

Going forward, you get to decide what maven means to you, and how you choose to embody that energy.

For now, I want you to know how proud I am of you. For everything you have accomplished and overcome. For how you choose to show up in the world.

And most importantly, I want to remind you that you had everything you needed within you the entire time.

You allowed yourself to be open to the teachers and the messages that this book offered, but you did the work.

You read the book.

As Paulo Coelho says in *The Alchemist*, "I only invoked what you already knew."

5

Remember your wisdom, embrace your magic and awaken the maven within you.

You are a maven.

In that, I honour all that you have been, all that you are becoming and all that you are.

Enjoy the journey.

AFTERWORD

Why am I doing what I'm doing? Because I don't think anyone should live a mediocre life if they don't want to. If there is any piece of you or your soul that is calling you to discover more depth, more richness and more understanding of yourself, and the life you desire, you deserve to follow that. If you feel like there's a piece of your puzzle missing, I hope this has sparked some inspiration and offered guidance to help you discover your next piece!

Part of my purpose and passion is in helping people awaken personally and spiritually. I want to awaken others to the potential of *their* possibilities. Anything and everything is possible. My hope is to remind you to have confidence in who you are. As the maven that you are. To remind you that this journey of becoming is a life-long journey – there is no end destination. And that's kind of the point, this whole journey is what makes up your life. In the moments, the stories and the learnings you are forever evolving and becoming more of a maven in your own life. And simultaneously, you are already there. You are a maven.

"To be all that I am. To show up exactly as I am,
vulnerable enough to allow myself to get hurt,
but courageous enough to keep going."
Ruth Montgomery

ACKNOWLEDGEMENTS

A special thanks to my mentors over the years; Jeanette, Harriette, Rebecca, Jennie, Diane, Morgan, Therese – you have all helped me more than you will ever know!

To my editorial cheerleaders – thank you for believing in me! I could not have done this without your support, assistance and encouragement along the way. Thank you: Candis, Ashley, Kiley, Leslee, Robin, Mackenzie, Jean and Staci.

And of course, to my family – Ian, Jean, Murray and Robin. Thank you for being there through this journey. From reviewing, helping keep me focused, looking after Sophie while I traveled to write this, and celebrating the little milestones along the way. Your support through my entrepreneurial journey means the world to me and thanks doesn't do it justice – I got so lucky when I got you as my family. We chose well!

ABOUT THE AUTHOR

Ruth Montgomery has had many titles over the years, including author, speaker, teacher, coach, event facilitator, and oracle deck co-creator. She is trained in Reiki, Somatic Experiencing, and Akashic Records. Her favourite titles however, are "collector of experiences" and "connector of people". She is here to experience all that life has to offer and in doing so, loves nothing more than to teach and share her experiences. She loves to travel and explore different parts of the world and calls Southwestern Ontario in Canada home, where she lives with her miniature pig, Sophie.

You can find Ruth at:
www.themavenproject.ca
or on Instagram at @themavenproject

JOURNAL PROMPTS FROM BOOK

Journal Prompts to Connect to Your Inner Child:

1. What did you love doing as a kid?
2. What did you used to spend your time doing?
3. What did you want to be when you grew up?
4. What are you passionate about now?
5. What have you always wanted to try?
6. What does happiness mean to you?
7. What do you love to do?
8. Where in your life can you be more creative?
9. What do you know to be true?
10. If you could go back, what would you tell 7-year-old you?
11. If you could go back, what would you tell 15-year-old you?

Journal Prompts for Cord Cutting:

1. Who do I need to forgive?
2. What experiences do I need to forgive?
3. What am I ready to release?

Journal Prompts for Self-Awareness:

1. What in your daily life excites you?
2. If money weren't a factor, how would you spend your days?
3. What are your strengths?
4. What are the traits you wish you could love more?
5. What do you admire in others that you wish you had?
6. What experiences do I need to forgive?
7. How am I holding myself back?
8. What do I love about myself?
9. What dream do I wish I could experience?
10. What is on my heart?
11. How do you want to feel?
12. How do you want to be remembered?
13. Are you currently living like you want to be remembered? What would you change?
14. What does happiness for other people, look like to you?
15. What does happiness for you, look like to you?

Journal Prompts for Dating Yourself:

1. Why are you judging yourself for that?
2. Would you judge someone else for that same thing?
3. What part of you felt vulnerable and insecure?
4. Did you feel unsafe?
5. Did it trigger something in you?
6. Where did you feel empowered?
7. Did that surprise you?
8. What did you do, that you wouldn't have thought you could do on your own?

Journal Prompts for Shadow Work:

1. Where do your shadows show up in emotions such as; selfishness, judgement, shame, need to control, temper tantrums, cockiness?
2. Where does this show up in my life?
3. What is this trying to teach me?
4. What is this trying to protect me from?
5. Where is this coming from?
6. Why am I responding this way?
7. Is this still serving me?
8. Is this true? If not, is it safe to release this shadow?

Journal Prompts Seasons of Identity:

1. Who am I?
2. What do I love about who I am?
3. Who were you when it was just you?
4. Who do you desire to be?
5. How do you desire to feel?
6. Who have I forgotten who I am?

Journal Prompts Seasons of Failure:

1. What did they teach you?
2. Who did they connect you with?
3. How did you react?
4. Would you do anything differently next time?
5. What am I supposed to learn from this?

REFERENCED & RECOMMENDED

To Read:

Alter, Adam. (2013). Drunk Tank Pink. New York, NY: Penguin Books.
Banayan, Alex. (2018). The Third Door. New York, NY: Crown Publishing Group.
Bernstein, Gabrielle. (2018). Judgement Detox. London, UK: Hay House UK Ltd.
Bernstein, Gabrielle. (2016). The Universe Has Your Back. United States: Hay House, Inc.
Brown, Brené. (2018). Dare to Lead. New York, NY: Random House.
Brown, Brené. (2010). Gifts of Imperfections. New York, NY: Random House.
Chapman, Gary. (1992). The 5 Love Languages. Chicago, IL: Northfield Publishing.
Coelho, Paulo. (1988). The Alchemist. San Francisco: HarperCollins.
Doyle, Glennon. (2020). Untamed. United States: The Dial Press.
Dyer, Dr. Wayne W. (2013). Wishes Fulfilled. United States: Hay House.
Echols, Damien. (2020). Angels & Archangels: A Magician's Guide. Boulder, CO: Sounds True.
Gilbert, Elizabeth. (2015). Big Magic. New York, NY: Bloomsbury Paperbacks.
Harder, Lori. (2018). A Tribe Called Bliss. New York, NY: Gallery Books.
Hay, Louise. (1984). You Can Heal Your Life. United States: Hay House, Inc.
Howes, Lewis. (2017). Mask of Masculinity. Pennsylvania, London, UK: Hay House UK Ltd.
Lister, Lisa. (2017). Witch. London, UK: Hay House UK Ltd.
Makichen, Walter. (2005). Spirit Babies. New York, NY: Bantam Dell.
Nester, James. (2020). Breath. New York, NY: Riverhead Books.
Segal, Inna. (2010). The Secret Language of Your Body. New York, NY: Atria Books/Beyond Words.
Singer, Michael. (2007). The Untethered Soul. Oakland, CA: New Harbinger Publications.
Thomashauer, Regena. (2016). Pussy: A Reclamation. United States: Hay House, Inc.
Watterson, Meggan. (2019). Mary Magdalene Revealed. United States of America: Hay House, Inc.
Westover, Tara. (2018). Educated. United States: Harper Collins Publishers.

To Watch: Derek Delgaudio's 'In And Of Itself'

To Listen: Please check the website, *www.themavenproject.ca/bamresources* for an audio meditation to Connect to Your Chakras, Source and to Ground your energy.

To Work With Ruth or Other Recommended Practitioners:

Please check the website, www.themavenproject.ca/bamresources for an updated list of the mavens and tools I would recommend.

Made in the USA
Las Vegas, NV
11 August 2024